They'll Be Okay

15 conversations to help your child through troubled times

Collett Smart

hachette
AUSTRALIA

hachette
AUSTRALIA

Published in Australia and New Zealand in 2019
by Hachette Australia
(an imprint of Hachette Australia Pty Limited)
Level 17, 207 Kent Street, Sydney NSW 2000
www.hachette.com.au

10 9 8 7 6 5 4 3 2 1

 A catalogue record for this
book is available from the
National Library of Australia

ISBN: 978 0 7336 4076 6 (paperback)

Cover design by Christabella Designs
Cover photograph courtesy of Getty Images
Author photo courtesy of Studio8
Text design by Kirby Jones
Typeset in Simoncini Garamond by Kirby Jones
Printed and bound in Australia by McPherson's Printing Group

To Greg,
my love, my life partner and my best friend.

CONTENTS

We are born to connect and communicate. We converse firstly through behaviour and eye contact. Then we add the language of music (think of the lilting oohs and ahhs of babies). Eventually we add words. As we develop, we become more skilled at interpreting the nuances of language – intonation, inflection, satire and humour.

Despite this innate drive to communicate, we live in a time of conversational impoverishment. We have plenty of likes and shares, we are bombarded with opinions and outrage, but the deep, enriching, art of *real* conversation is at risk of extinction.

The danger of this impoverishment is that we will miss out on the experience of being irrevocably altered by our encounters with other people.

There are more interesting things to do in life than look at yourself admiringly in the mirror or post selfies or hear your own opinion echoed back to you on social media. Conversations require more curiosity and thought, and less opinion and judgement.

Less involvement in conversations means we don't open ourselves as readily to the consideration of other perspectives, belief systems, values and attitudes. We also miss out on clarifying our own points of view and values. You may have had the experience of speaking to someone and hearing yourself say something you didn't know you believed or thought.

A single conversation can change a life. Perhaps you can think of a time when a comment so touched you, it echoed in your mind until it found a place in your heart. Perhaps there were words of comfort, support or understanding that you heard as a child that serve as a cloak against the chill winds of hurt that face us all from time to time. Even if you can't recall a conversation of this impact, you have had one. The reason you may not immediately remember it is that the words of the other person rang so truly they wove themselves into your heart and became a part of who you.

There is an African saying that people are people because of other people. What connects us to others is love and conversation. Great conversations are like enchanting songs sung between people. Conversations can harmonise, soothe, resonate and deepen our relationships.

The art of conversation

Our relationships have a tremendous impact on our happiness, and conversation is the glue that binds relationships together. Given how important conversations are, we should all set ourselves the goal of becoming better conversationalists, so that we can create meaningful and happy lives.

If you think of some of the wonderful conversations you have had it is probable that they had some of these features:

- People stopped what they were doing and really listened
- Curiosity was piqued
- Jealousy and competition were absent
- Differences were seen as interesting rather than threatening
- People felt able to be authentic and to show their vulnerabilities

- Hurts might have been talked about but faults were not
- Ideas and humour were played with.

In this wonderful book, *They'll Be Okay*, Collett Smart provides us with guidelines for fifteen essential conversations to have with children and teenagers. Given the comprehensive detail Collett has provided about what works, let me share with you some of the ways of conversing that definitely *don't* work:

The uninvited or unsolicited lecture

This is a quite compelling habit. You can feel like you are imparting wisdom or sharing the hard-earned lessons from the university of life. Using the wisdom of your years to put a wiser older head on younger shoulders.

Ha! Perhaps you've noticed if you provide the same lecture in the same way over and over again, you see the whites of their eyes. They stop listening to you.

Appeals for loyalty or common sense

After all we've done! Look how desperately worried we are! Anyone with sense… If they told you to jump off a cliff would you do it?

Wringing your hands and looking concerned is not going to carry the day.

Self-sacrifice or self-denial

This is the idea that parents should be martyrs who sacrifice their own lives to raise their kids.

One of the most powerful things parents can do to promote well-being in their children is to live life well themselves. Make sure your children and teens see you enjoying yourself, catching up with friends and taking time to have great conversations. Show teens that life is worth living and success is worth attaining.

Answering your own questions

At times teens can be so sullen and uncommunicative that you find yourself having a one-sided conversation in which you ask the questions and then fill in the answers as well. Be careful: this can sneak up on you. One day you walk away from a conversation with your teen and realise that only one person has said anything at all.

The fine art of talking, getting your message heard and understood as well as converted into action by another human being is an amazingly tricky business. When it is your own child or teenager you are trying to influence, the mission becomes even more challenging. Collett's wonderful book will help you navigate these challenges and guide you to create deep and meaningful conversations that will resonate and reverberate throughout your child's life.

Andrew Fuller
Clinical Psychologist

SECTION 1

Who, Why and What Matters?

CHAPTER 1

Helping kids flourish

If you wandered down my street you would probably discover that we are the loud house on the corner. I think families have personalities, just like individuals have a personality, and my family's personality traits include passionate, loud and affectionate. We certainly have other traits – but these are what might hit you first. Most of what we do is like this. We play and have fun loudly, debate and argue issues passionately, show affection enthusiastically (think rough-and-tumble play, and jostling for bear hugs), and we say sorry – a lot. My eldest son has finished school, my daughter is in the thick of high school and my younger son is in late primary school and, like any parents, my husband and I are living the daily joys and challenges that parenthood brings. Kids are the same as they have always been; the only difference for us as parents, in this age, is that we need to navigate an added dimension. That is, we're raising children in a technological age.

As both a school teacher and a psychologist I have had the privilege of working with young people, their parents and their schools, on different continents, for over 20 years. Technology means we are members of a global village. The same technology challenges faced by parents and teachers in Australian cities are those of the rural communities in Zimbabwe or the Philippines, where mobile phone data top-up 'scratchies' can be bought by children for a few dollars on street corners. When parents talk to me after my parenting seminars every week, they want to know that they are not alone in trying to effectively wrestle the risks that technology ushers into their homes, while building on the benefits it brings. I hear these same discussions among parents in any city or continent I happen to be working in. My own home is certainly not immune to the negotiating and juggling and trying to figure out what is helpful and what is harmful. Why would it be? We're a normal family who use technology on a daily basis.

Despite the fantastic benefits of technology in the areas of social connectivity, access to educational resources and easy entertainment, there is one area in particular that has the potential to detrimentally affect the psychological and social development of this generation of young people: porn culture. It is a culture of objectification which affects the way we value others and the way we see ourselves.

So I began to ask questions. I wanted to know what parents and teachers wanted to know about raising their children in this #metoo climate.

What parents want to know

Many told me that they felt overwhelmed and bombarded by the terrible stories and statistics on pornography, harassment and bullying, yet they had very little information about what they might practically do to support the children in their own homes and classrooms. Countless people asked me a variation of these two questions: 'How do I teach my child about healthy relationships?' and 'When young people are bombarded by destructive media messages on a daily basis, can we really make a difference?' I realised they wanted to know *how* to make a practical difference in the day-to-day stuff of their child's life.

It dawned on me then that although there were many wonderful talks, that raised awareness of the problem of objectification and porn culture, no one was giving parents advice on how to tackle these issues and teach healthy relationships at each age and stage of their child's development. I realised that parents need hope. They need to believe that despite the statistics or the perceived enormity of any situation – **there is always hope**. A positive spark, no matter how small, will fuel the belief that there is something that can be done, by us everyday parents, with our everyday children, in our everyday relationships.

Can we really make a difference?

I think I have the best job in the world, because I get to work with teenagers – a lot. I really love young people. It's true! I find them to be deep thinkers, unafraid to question ideas and eager to make a difference in their world. Many are passionate about causes and are loyal friends. We must invest in young people. They are our future MPs, filmmakers, teachers, policy makers, parents ... These are the people who will take over the macro-level battles. Who will continue to lobby governments for change, take on the technology companies for their lack of social responsibility, put pressure on advertising and film industries that normalise toxic culture, and call out retail industries that exploit women and children for profit. They will be the ones with the power to make big changes to what is and make it what it should be. I know this to be true because I am often deeply moved by the questions of young people who want to know how they might start a movement or a cause that can make a positive difference. But while they learn about themselves, others and their culture, our young people need adults who listen and support them, and model how to do this *now*.

Primary caregivers are the first and most predominant role models in children's lives. Although children make their own choices, carers play a significant role in helping to shape and mould the attitudes, ethical development and resilience of young people as they grow. Researchers have repeatedly stressed that social and educational strategies are the most effective ones we have for minimising the harms associated with children's exposure to porn culture. The top three strategies include:

1. parental understanding and monitoring;
2. teaching children media literacy and skills in critical analysis of media messages; and
3. providing alternative content on sexuality to young people – content that is compelling and educational, and which includes materials on sex and relationships.[1, 2]

Although technological solutions are vital, these strategies may be more effective over the long term, and have the potential to minimise the negative effects of exposure when it does occur.

Yet we still collectively avoid the topics of sexualised and pornographic images and their effects on youth development. Perhaps because they are awkward topics? Perhaps we're afraid of offending some parents in the school's audience who are facing their own issues? We no longer shy away from teaching about the risks of underage drinking, smoking or drug use, and we aren't worried about offending the carer in the audience who might have their own alcohol issues. Why? Because we know that these things pose great risk to our children's development and wellbeing. So **our children need us to get over ourselves**. They need brave mentors who are willing to push through our own baggage and discomfort to advocate for them, guide them and show them an alternative.

Every parent wishes for their child to have meaningful relationships and to grow into a person who can both give and receive love. In a world bombarded with sexualised images and conflicting online messages about love, we need a new conversation with young people.

The good news is that the conversation is not as difficult as we imagine it to be. I believe the way to tackle this porn crisis is head on, by **fighting for love**. And love is exactly what young people say they *want* to know more about. We spend so much time worrying about how to have 'the sex talk' that we don't realise that 'the love talk' might be the more important conversation to have with young people. They sit up and take notice when we talk about how to do relationships well, yet this is still something we do little to prepare them for. If we begin early and frame our discussions around love, empathy, kindness, compassion, body safety and self-care within the context of relationships, we arm children with a much broader life skillset. Indeed, for young people to identify what an unhealthy relationship looks like, they first need to know and be able to recognise what healthy relationships look like.

This book is for those who have said to me, 'I know there's a problem, but what now?' and 'While we continue to lobby government bodies and put pressure on media industries to catch up, what can I do to support the child in my personal world?' It is a tool for helping relationships to flourish, despite a world marinating in online abuse material. It is a handbook for starting ethical conversations and strengthening trust between you and your children, from two to teens, as you tackle the tough topics of life.

Don't worry: these topics don't need to be covered in one sitting, or even one year. Rather, they will be conversations over the course of your child's journey to adulthood. Of course there will be challenging times, with some struggling more than others. Particular periods may be difficult – really difficult, but anywhere there is a bunch of humans living in a confined space it's never going to be easy. There will be days (maybe even weeks) when you second guess yourself, and wonder, *Am I doing this right?*, *Will they be okay?* Hold strong. I believe in the potential of this generation. For the most part – **they'll be okay!**

Join me as we raise a thriving generation who will know how to love and be loved.

CHAPTER 2

Strong relationships are where healthy conversations thrive

The good life is built with good relationships.

– Robert Waldinger

One thing that continually strikes me about the young people I work with is that they really do want to become good men and women who have rich, meaningful relationships – they are just not sure how to go about it. Many are turning to the internet for both connection and advice, yet despite the wealth of information out there, what they get is not always accurate. Nuances in relationships, body language and, of course, sex are as difficult to decipher through a website as they ever were from a textbook or magazine. Young people need affirmation and unconditional love; information about healthy and unhealthy behaviours; clarity about values such as respect and integrity, appropriate boundaries and limits, and guidance about making responsible, safe choices.

I believe we are made for relationships. Modelling what healthy relationships look like is, in my opinion, the most vital skill we can teach our children.

A 75-year landmark study on men's relationships and wellness supports this view.[1] It revealed that early fame, wealth and high achievement don't bring happiness. The study concluded that social connections are really good for us and loneliness kills; people who are more connected to family, to friends, to community are happier, physically healthier and live longer, while lonely people are less happy, their health declines earlier in midlife, their brain functioning declines sooner, and they live shorter lives than people who are not lonely. In his TED Talk based on this study, psychiatrist Robert Waldinger concludes, 'Good relationships keep us happier and healthier, period.' Other studies show lack of social connection is more detrimental to health than obesity, smoking and high blood pressure.

It is important to note that it is not the number of friends you have, or whether or not you are in a romantic relationship, that matters but the *quality* of your close relationships. Having good relationships is the protective factor. In general, people who feel more connected to others have higher self-esteem, possess greater empathy, and are more trusting and cooperative.

What has all this to do with porn culture? We know our children are growing up bombarded by messages that celebrate selfishness. Porn culture focuses on 'me' and 'my pleasure' and 'my sexual satisfaction', to the exclusion of relationships or intimacy or a healthy self-worth. A 'me, me, me' porn culture is directly opposed to empathy. Pornography models how to use and objectify others as a means to satisfy the physical self. My colleagues and I see the negative effects of pornography consumption on young people every week. It leads to isolation and erodes their innate human ability for healthy social connection.

Who matters to young people and why?

If relationships are the key protective factor for both mental and physical health, then adults should invest in modelling healthy relationships to children. I believe that our most effective weapon against the destructive impacts of porn and violence is to engage with and teach our children about empathy within healthy relationships. Countless studies indicate that one of the key factors that build resilience in young people is a sense of being connected to adults. It is within these relationships that we teach, inspire, connect, and also model to our young people how to care for others. I believe our role as parents is to raise children who will contribute positively not only to our own family but also to the wider world – who will fight for a greater good, raise awareness about injustice facing the weak and implore government bodies to act on their behalf. Children look to us for authoritative guidance and it is our responsibility to guide them with firm boundaries, high expectations and truckloads of love and acceptance. The purpose of creating scaffolding for our children is not to restrict their every movement or choice but to allow for a wealth of opportunity and development of resilience, while offering protection. This provides a better quality of life for them and those around them.

The fact kids are not all succumbing to forced or unhappy sex too young, or too drunk, or with too many different people – didn't happen by chance. A pitched battle is taking place with concerted efforts from educators, parents and groups such as Collective Shout, against the uncaring and downright exploitive marketers and the tendency of some parents to put their heads in the sand about the flood of pornography and meanness that the internet brings. If the kids are OK, it's because some adults never lost sight of the need to advocate for them, defend them, educate them, and give them the self-belief to choose wisely and well.

– Steve Biddulph, 2014, *Sydney Morning Herald*,
commenting on a La Trobe study

We are in this for the long haul

Our children learn values from the adults they spend the most time with in both the day-to-day joys *and* the struggles. For children to build healthy relationships requires the adults in their lives to make use of effective communication skills and age-appropriate boundaries. Without purposeful conversations and intentional activities with our children, they will be lost (see Chapter 4 for age-related ideas). I see too many teens who are hurting assume that coming of age involves lots of meaningless sex, alcohol and reckless behaviour, without any thought of consequences.

The problem is, as humans, we often want a quick fix, especially for issues like dealing with porn culture. We want things to be instant (like our coffee pods), but relationships are hard work and messy. We are in a time when we need to open up and have conversations that we possibly never had with our own parents. Sex education has changed dramatically since we were young, because it has been forced to. It is no longer just 'the talk'. Today it is about lots of small, frequent, repetitive conversations, in the context of healthy relationships. These conversations can only happen if adults continue to build a climate of trust and openness, where children feel comfortable coming to us for answers, and where no topic is off limits. Trust me, if the adults in their lives are not talking to them, the internet will be. I'm not sure about you, but I want to get in before Google does.

We've all heard the saying 'knowledge is power', but with our newfound easy access to information we are all suffering overload. Simply possessing knowledge is not equal to having wisdom. Wisdom develops by wrestling with, debating and critically thinking about what we hear, see and read. With the right knowledge, children will have an expanded capacity to understand that the changes they are going through are positive and dynamic, and part of becoming a healthy, capable adult.

Of course, having good information doesn't mean things won't get messy – things will get very messy at times – but with your help young people will have the capacity to navigate around the mess. In the words of psychology blogger Karen Young, 'Think of it like switching on a light in a darkened room. The obstacles will still be there – right in the middle of where they need to walk, but when they can see what's happening they will have a better chance of navigating around those obstacles, rather than falling over them.'

I'm sure that, right about now, some readers might be freaking out a little and thinking, 'But kids don't want to hear that stuff from their parents! They will probably stick their fingers in their ears and go "la-la-la".' However, despite what we hear about the current generation gap and terms like 'screenagers', 'technology dinosaurs' and 'the iGeneration', Mission Australia's annual surveys of thousands of young people consistently indicate '*friendships* and *family relationships* ranked as their two most highly valued items'.[2] While, '*friend/s, parent/s and relatives/ family friends*' were the three most commonly cited sources of help for young people – higher than the internet!

A review of more than three decades of research[3] indicates a strong link between good communication between parents and children, and young people making more responsible choices around sexual behaviours and even engaging in less pornography use. But the most recent studies show that we need to go further than just talking about the mechanics of sex. As one teen said, 'All we are taught is how to prevent stuff, how not to get pregnant. We should be discussing the values that should guide you in love and how to really love and respect someone else. And how to be loved by someone else. That's a lot more important.' Teens want us to talk about the tender, subtle, life-giving stuff of learning how to love and be loved, and how to develop a mature romantic relationship.[4]

There it is – your children *want* to hear from you!

Connection matters

Naturally, forging connections with kids is the same as for anyone – they need our *time*. Spending time with and meeting them where they are at is crucial to our children's healthy development. This is not a new secret in terms of how to relate to children, nor is it specific for only young children. There are positive associations for teens who spend an average of six hours a week engaged in family time with their parents. The more time teens spend in family time – such as during meals, having a parent watching them play sport, driving to guitar lessons, attending Grandma's birthday, popping up to the shop together, on holidays, chatting after a party – the less likely they are to abuse drugs and alcohol and engage in other risky or illegal behaviour.[5] Many parents (even working mums) are spending more time with their kids than in past generations.[6] So despite what we hear about teenagers, even when they push us away, they need our time just as much as they did when they were 5 years old, just in a different way.

Be who they need

Children look to adults for authoritative guidance and should certainly be given more independence and choice as they grow, like crossing the street, catching a train on their own, or riding a bicycle up to the shops. Yet, they are not fully functioning adults and do not have the life experience or the wisdom to navigate certain areas of life on their own. We know from studies of the brain that the prefrontal cortex, which is the area of the brain that enables us to plan, consider, control impulses and make wise judgements, is underdeveloped in children and teens, so they still need adult guidance (which is different from control) as they learn to make healthy choices. They don't need us to simply be a 40-year-old BFF (Best Friend Forever).

With this in mind, let's have a closer look at the various adults who can influence a child's life.

Parents

For almost a century we've formally recognised the psychological and emotional benefits of attachment between a child and a primary caregiver. However, we need to be careful that we don't only think of beneficial attachment in terms of a Western worldview. Many cultures have different ways of developing a healthy attachment to their children. What children everywhere have in common is the need for love – in some ways, they crave it as much as (or even more than) basic needs like food. We now know that children who do not develop secure attachments can develop something called 'rejection sensitivity'.[7] This includes a hyper-alertness to the social reactions of other people. When someone has rejection sensitivity they consistently expect, look out for and overreact to any forms of perceived rejection. They fear rejection and come to anxiously expect it, but then rapidly overreact to any perceived form of it, often misinterpreting or distorting the actions of another person. Those with rejection sensitivity are at a greater risk of initiating violence against a romantic partner. The good news is that people can learn how to develop healthy relationships.

Parenting styles still count in the technological age

The four parenting styles recognised by experts are Authoritarian, Permissive, Authoritative and Neglectful. These are easily applied to all aspects of parenting, including boundaries with technology use. What we learned from the research on parenting styles is that children thrive best under the care of an Authoritative parenting style, and that this style works well for families, regardless of their ethnicity, income, education or structure. Helping your child to develop a secure attachment does not mean you need to act like a friend or give in to all of their demands.

Authoritarian parents value obedience and conformity to rules, and they tend to be punitive, inflexible and controlling of their children, while Permissive parents are reluctant to impose rules or set standards, and prefer to let their children regulate themselves – they are the 'peerant' rather than the parent. Neglectful parents have the least amount of involvement or response towards their children's physical and emotional needs. Some may provide basic food and shelter, but are emotionally detached, indifferent and even oblivious to a child's needs, and do not bother about boundaries. In contrast, an Authoritative parent is assertive and has clear standards of behaviour for their children, while simultaneously trying to be supportive and understanding of their children's point of view. Authoritative parents still set limits, but also reason with their children and are responsive to their emotional needs.

Children raised with Authoritative parenting are the most psychologically well adjusted and intrinsically motivated to achieve. They manage themselves well, are self-reliant and self-confident, more resilient and have good self-control. They have good social skills and remain connected to parents and friends. This is exactly the type of young person we want sitting at the table at breakfast or behind a screen in another room.

It is this style of parenting that we ought to strive for as we talk with our children about their technology use and the content they might be exposed to. The platform does not change the ethic. Taking the Authoritarian route and locking all devices away or banning social media until they are 18 (yes, I had a parent proudly tell me that was their philosophy) simply sets up our children for future failure. Simultaneously, taking a Permissive role and throwing our hands up in despair, shutting our eyes and hoping they will be okay, opens children up to all manner of current and future psychological and social issues.

Reassuringly, research tells us that a warm and communicative parent–child relationship (Authoritative style) is the most important factor in reducing porn use among children.

The role of fathers

There is so much to say about the role of fathers and what 'fathering' actually means that this section could fill an entire book on its own. In fact, it already has. Thanks to the work of Steve Biddulph and others, the role of the modern father has changed dramatically in the last generation. Contrary to beliefs of old, a child needs to bond with *both* parents, not only their mother. It is a father's duty to nurture his children and make sure they feel loved, not just once they become teens but from the minute they are born. The more time a father spends with his children, the stronger their bond will become. The great news is that many fathers are more engaged and involved with their children than ever, with studies[8] showing that dads who live with their kids have tripled the amount of time they spend with them compared with 50 years ago.

Numerous studies on the role of fathers show that dads – whether married or single – matter a lot.[9, 10] Fathers who spend quality time with their children help instil self-control and social skills[11] and even influence academic achievement. One report[12] indicates that many dads engage in more play with their children than mums do (perhaps because mums, in general, still tend to carry more of the day-to-day household load).

As the first male directly involved in a child's life, Dad will model what it means to be a man. Research shows that when a daughter has a secure, supportive and communicative relationship with her dad, she is more likely to create and maintain emotionally intimate, fulfilling relationships with men.[13] Most encouragingly, a close relationship with Dad can lead to daughters being more assertive and self-confident in refusing to have sex when they do not wish to, as well as refusing to be emotionally dominated by their partners.[14] Various studies indicate that father support has been associated with a reduction in sexual risk behaviours in both adolescent sons and daughters.[15, 16, 17]

Through Dad, both sons and daughters learn about what men value about themselves and what they value in women. This happens in the conversations a father has with his daughters and sons, what he communicates about their value, how he talks about his partner and how he refers to his children's mother.

Dad also communicates family values when he talks about or refers to other women in front of his children, even when he thinks they are not listening. In other words, fathers have a very strong influence on how their children interpret the roles of women and react to rape culture.

Research indicates that children need dads to show up emotionally, every day, to love them and model appropriate behaviour.[18] Father-absence creates a gaping emotional need for belonging and acceptance in children that they will try to fill in some other way – with drugs, alcohol, sex, gangs or porn. For boys, healthy manhood doesn't just happen – it *must* be taught. Men need to invest in boys' lives early on, and earn the right to walk them through the tumultuous teen years, to have conversations about relationships, intimacy, sex and porn.

The role of mothers

There's no way to be a perfect mother and a million ways to be a good one.

– Jill Churchill, author

A mother, more often in the role of primary caregiver, is incredibly important in a child's development. We know that a mother's touch, warmth and responsiveness all affect a child's physical, psychological and social wellbeing. More recent research proves that it has a significant impact on brain size. Children whose mothers were nurturing and provided emotional support in their preschool years were found to have more growth in the hippocampus, which is associated with learning, memories and regulating emotions.[19] And this growth trajectory was associated with healthier emotional functioning when the children entered their teen years. So the manner in which mothers might respond to children's wants and needs shape how they interact with others, respond to strangers and explore their environments, which ends up playing a massive role in how children learn and grow throughout their entire lives. Additionally, the more time a teen spends engaged with their mother, the fewer instances of delinquent behaviour occur.

Hence, attachments with mothers plays a significant role in the lives of children and teens. Mothers have a unique opportunity to teach their sons about girls, how to treat them and how to get along with them. Mums also model to their daughters what 'value' and 'worth' look like, and how we should expect other people to respond to us within close relationships. These messages shape what young people will look for and how they will treat romantic partners, friends and colleagues.

I would like to do a shout-out to the single mums here. There are so many single mothers carrying a huge parenting load and doing a brilliant job with their children. To these mums, make time to look after yourself too and make sure you fill your own tank regularly with rest, time with girlfriends and an activity you love – it is better for both you and your children when you do.

Mentors

Make wisdom human to the adolescent mind.
> – Will Durant, writer, historian and philosopher

In the section on dads, I mentioned that boys need men to model to them what a healthy man looks like. Some boys, however, may not have a father in their lives. I have the privilege of working with some incredible single mums, yet it is imperative that single mothers of boys actively encourage the support of real-life, positive, trusted male role models in their sons' lives.

There is often a father figure or father-like substitute (a sports coach, a teacher, a youth leader, a grandparent, an uncle) who can step into this space. Indeed, they must, if we are ever to break the cycle of violence and inadequacy from being handed from one generation to another. Of course, in our girls' lives, older women can step in as surrogate grandparents and aunties, and also provide a place of advice, support and example.

There is strong support for the benefits of role models. A five-year study in Canada found that children with positive mentors were more confident, had fewer behavioural problems, showed increased belief in their abilities to succeed in school and felt less anxiety related to peer pressure.[20] Girls were found to be four times less likely to become bullies and boys were two times less likely to become bullies.

Community is so important! It is unnatural to try to raise a child alone, yet with the breakdown of family and the urbanisation of culture we are driven into isolation more than ever. Both parents and their children need others for support. In a community we look out for each other's children and our own problems tend to fall into perspective. Community is something we ought to be conscious of and work towards building. Our children's health depends on it.

Community

> It takes a whole *village to raise a child.*
>
> – Igbo and Yoruba (Nigerian) proverb

The above well-known village proverb exists, in different forms, in many African languages. Growing up in South Africa, I learned to speak fluent Zulu – I was even a Zulu teacher for a time – and heard a variation of it often. In the West we tend to romanticise the proverb a little, with politicians quoting it to convey their dedication to children, and so on. However, the essence of this proverb comes from the fact that African – and Asian, and

Central and South American – cultures are largely collectivistic, while Western cultures are more individualistic. In a collectivistic culture, raising a child is a communal effort and should be shared by the larger family and the *whole* village (aunties, youth workers, teachers, the butcher, the baker, the candlestick maker – you get the idea). Ideally, all the adults in a community take care of and look out for other people's children, and the children are expected to show respect for and learn from the wisdom of the elders.

Most collectivistic cultures place greater value on one's group and the goal of social life is to harmonise with and support one's community. They nurture what is called the interdependent self. For example, it is an African custom to greet a person by their family or clan name, as this is a recognition that one doesn't arrive at personhood without the influence of those around us. The village incorporates the southern African philosophy of *Ubuntu* – meaning 'A person is a person through other people'. Ubuntu recognises that we are formed through the influence and care of and interaction with our 'tribe'. We do not exist in isolation and did not arrive at who we are by our own making. Ubuntu acknowledges our interconnectedness – that what we do also affects the world around us. In contrast, the psychology of individualistic culture assumes that our lives are enriched by relying on the power of our personal control, enhancing our individual selves and making choices independently.

Obviously, sentimentalising one or the other is not the point here, because with globalisation and the fragmentation of society we will find individualism and collectivism vary from person to person and culture to culture. There is, however, something to be learned from the sense of community that traditional collectivistic cultures bring. As the research indicates, social support increases physical health and psychological wellbeing. We are social creatures and our psychological and physical health will suffer if we lack fulfilling, caring relationships and meaningful connections to a larger community – our 'tribe'.

What community might look like

You can't be human all by yourself, and when you have
this quality – Ubuntu – you are known for your generosity.
We think of ourselves far too frequently as just individuals,
separated from one another, whereas you are connected and
what you do affects the whole world. When you do well, it
spreads out; it is for the whole of humanity.

– Desmond Tutu

We live in a time when children are bombarded with more alternative voices of authority than ever. These voices come from the online world, television, school, friends and advertising. The technology that fills their lives (and ours) and which was intended to connect us can sometimes separate us. Part of the solution may be to intentionally think about ways in which we can raise children in community, rather than in isolation. But what does this look like in real life? A strong, vibrant community surrounding a child might include elders who support parents, and parents who are open to seeking advice and help from elders. It might involve other parents, parents of our children's friends, aunties, uncles and grandparents who support the values created in our homes. It should also include partnerships with schools, where teachers, boarding-house staff, counsellors and heads of school are held accountable and seen as allies in raising whole families. Trusted mentors who are active in our neighbourhoods, churches and sports clubs and who support the teaching of values, such as respecting others and respecting property, are also important. This is community.

To build community requires risk and sacrifice. It requires slowing down and intentionally connecting with others. It is in the intentional conversations and interactions with others that relationships grow. It is in community that children learn to value people above possessions and see every human being as precious – because children believe your actions more than they believe your words, because 'a person is a person through other people'.

If you are an introvert and you are reading this, fear not, for I am the queen of introverts. Connection doesn't mean you have to go out and be the life of the party (or community); it simply means reciprocating care and showing kindness, even to one struggling teen or one single mum.

*

A final word of advice: in this age of paedophile-fuelled porn we should rightly be mindful when our children are around other adults on their own. I do believe that constant fears of abuse can rob our children of the relationships they need and crave to be able to grow into strong, emotional, sensitive and affectionate men and women. Yet, remember that predators also groom families, not just the child. So if you have engaged the support of a mentor in your son's or daughter's life, don't be afraid to ask lots of questions (of your child and of the mentor). Ask the adult to run conversation topics past you first, so that you know what they are chatting about with your child. If an adult gets offended and says you don't trust them, then they are not the right person for your child. Make sure you provide your child with body safety and personal boundaries language (see more in Conversation #1), and request that any engagement be in a public space. And if you have a personal history that involves abuse, know that you may want to seek the input and advice of others you trust, to help correctly judge the character and motives of mentors. Don't be afraid to openly ask others for their thoughts about the mentor's character, but also learn to hone and trust your own instincts.

Key Messages

- Social connections are really good for us and loneliness kills.
- Good communication between parents and children means young people make more responsible choices around sexual behaviours and engage in less pornography use.
- Children thrive best under the care of an Authoritative parenting style. Children raised this way are the most psychologically well adjusted and are self-reliant and self-confident, and have good self-control.
- Children need to bond with *both* parents: fathers help instil self-control and social skills, and a mother's touch, warmth and responsiveness all affect a child's physical, psychological and social wellbeing.
- We are social creatures and our psychological and physical health will suffer if we lack fulfilling, caring relationships and meaningful connections to a larger community.

CHAPTER 3

7 tips for a firm foundation to build conversations upon

I begin my seminars by asking parents, 'What do you wish for your child's future adult?' And then I add, 'Please say something besides "to be happy".' I get confused looks. I'm a psychologist – isn't my job supposed to be one that leads people to live happier lives? I follow my question by showing this quote:

> *The purpose of life is not to be happy. It is to be useful, to be honourable, to be compassionate, to have it make some difference that you have lived and lived well.*
>
> – Ralph Waldo Emerson

It is not that I intend for people to be *unhappy*. I don't want your children to be sad. Goodness, I don't want *my* children to be sad! But happiness is a funny thing – the more we try to pursue it directly, the more it tends to elude us. Indeed, no child whoops with happiness when asked to unpack the dishwasher. Come to think of it, I definitely don't jump for joy when unpacking the dishwasher. Dishwasher unpacking certainly isn't up there on the top of anyone's bucket list! Neither is studying for exams, or travelling to work by bus in the pouring rain without an umbrella. Some things don't bring about feelings of immediate happiness, but they are necessary and show responsibility, develop perseverance and character. The full gamut of emotion is what makes us human. Feeling emotions other than happiness is part of life, part of being human. Feelings pass and we learn from and develop character through the 'un-fun' times.

Yes, 'character' – that's what I mean when I talk about having a vision for your child's 'future adult'. I don't mean specifically trying to channel a child onto a career path or into a particular relationship. I mean having a vision for the values you want to instil in your child. A vision of a future adult with an understanding of consequences, selfless love, empathy, boundaries, consent and intimacy. An adult who treats others with compassion and respect. Even the new popular positive psychology movement is not a form of 'happy-ology'. Positive psychology is aimed at helping people flourish and two of the main aims remain others-focused. These include being able to engage and relate to other people, and to look beyond oneself and help others to find lasting meaning, satisfaction and wisdom. When we teach children to value others and relationships, happiness arrives as a by-product.

Essentially, if we teach children to become love-ABLE rather than simply loveable, to learn that other people have worth also, this is when they truly thrive. Within this framework, here are 7 tips to help parents lay a firm foundation on which to build their future conversations about relationships, love and even sex.

1. Start with a parenting mantra

When we have a parenting mantra, we are more likely to follow through (or not follow through) with certain decisions as we raise our children. We are also more likely to behave in certain ways ourselves, because we know that 'do as I say, not as I do' is simply unacceptable. To paraphrase Marian Wright Edelman, an American activist for the rights of children, 'Children cannot be what they cannot see.' In other words, we are only as good as the men and women we have known and seen. Hence my mantra: 'Parent with your child's future adult in mind.' This is not about micromanaging every aspect of a child's life, it is about the broader parenting decisions that govern the day-to-day routines and interactions as we raise whole children and whole families. Your mantra might be different from mine, but a mantra usually involves coming up with a phrase that summarises the intentions behind your parenting decisions and includes thinking about what you hope to develop in your child's character. A mantra springs from our love for our children but isn't Authoritarian. Your mantra is often best when you are sure of your main family values.

2. Know your values

What three values do you believe are most important to your family? Any of your top three values might include: respect, kindness, love, self-control, humility, compassion, justice, selflessness, peace, patience, honesty. For example, my closest friend's main family value is kindness. She regularly reminds her children of the phrase, 'In the future, people won't remember anything about you, other than how they *felt* when they were around you. Remember to be kind.'

Try to find ways to make your values visible. We have an image hanging on a wall in our lounge, with the words, 'Think deeply, speak gently, love much, laugh a lot, work hard, give freely and be kind.' There are many such images available in shops and online. Perhaps you could find one that most closely represents your values and hang it where your family sees it every day?

Use your values as the foundation for your family discussions. It is through their relationships with their parents that children learn what is important and how to treat others. Also know that despite our children acting as though they don't hear them, or even appear to flat-out reject them, when our values are communicated within warm loving relationships, most children hold them as central once they become adults.[1]

It should go without saying that all discussion becomes moot if we don't watch our own words and actions. We cannot expect children to behave empathically, respectfully or make wise choices if the very models they live with communicate the opposite. So before we even start talking to children about sex or porn culture, we need to model our values in everyday encounters. Children are watching how we talk to the elderly lady at the post office, how we refer to the women at the local gym, how we treat younger children, how we support the boy with a disability and how we speak to our partners. They also notice if we mess up and apologise and try to do better the next time. This teaches them that we will all make mistakes in our relationships, but we learn from those mistakes and do our best to change our behaviour when it hurts ourselves or others. The challenge to us adults is: what might we need to start doing differently from here on?

3. Stow away your own baggage on sexuality

We know that we need to talk to our children about sexuality, but many parents feel uncertain or anxious about how to bring up sexual themes. Parents tell me that they grew up in an era when mentioning sex was the unspoken taboo at home. But, if you dared, you would receive a brief clinical talk on the biology of where babies come from or have a book surreptitiously left on your bed – conversation closed! Your parents' body language and discomfort led you to intuitively discern that you should never bring up that topic again. So as parents now ourselves, with that message seared into our brains, it is important to be aware of the baggage that we bring into conversations with our own children about sexuality. Be encouraged and be kind to yourself – we've come a long way. My mum's generation grew up thinking they were dying at the sight of their first period, so our parents were doing better than their own parents in this area, and so will we.

4. Early and often

As parents, we are often afraid of getting it wrong, giving too much information or basically not knowing how to start. So we say nothing at all, and fail to build a crucial area of our children's lives. Young children will talk about sexuality as openly as what they had for lunch at preschool. We need to shove aside our baggage, take our children's lead and launch into it – at age-appropriate levels, of course.

None of this is about one sit-down conversation. Rather, regular chats at each age and stage of your children's lives are what they need. As you begin to talk through these issues with your children, you not only equip them with the information they need to make wise choices, but your relationship with them deepens, and they learn that they can trust you in the most sensitive areas of life. In addressing any of the issues in this book, we must not lose sight of the fact that sexual curiosity is a normal aspect of being a young person. In every conversation, we need to work at dispelling awkwardness and to reassure kids and teens that they are not weird because they want to know about their bodies or sexual encounters.

At every stage:

Step 1: Breathe and be prepared. When your bub is born, you can hardly imagine your new bundle of joy one day wondering out loud, at the dinner table in front of your boss, why others in their year 5 class giggled when the answer to a maths problem turned out to be 69 (true story)! Figure out what you believe and where you stand on various topics. This is vital to supporting young people when they come to you with questions. Listen and talk to other young people, where possible, to find out their views, debate topics with other adults and read widely, so that you become comfortable with your own views as well as learning to respect the views of others, including your child's. If you have a partner, you need to talk about your established values (see

Section 2 on page 26), what you believe and how you are going to handle topics as they arise, before they do. Obviously new things will pop up along the way, but you need to be clear on some of the fundamentals of your beliefs and then parent as a team.

Step 2: Make use of opportunities that present themselves at different stages. Use any opportunity to communicate your shared values as a family (see below for more ideas on this). Children need to regularly hear and see what you believe in an obvious manner. They can't know what you believe if you don't show and tell them.

Step 3: When discussing topics such as media messages, billboard messages, online content or sex and relationships in general, find out what your children actually know. In the event they have mistaken ideas or facts, you will be able to correct any misconceptions. And you'll avoid launching into a long explanation of something a child was not referring to in the first place.

TRY THIS:

'Can you tell me more about what you mean when you say ...?'

Step 4: Attempt to answer any questions simply but honestly, and in a reassuring way. The key is to keep your responses appropriate to the age of your child and also in line with your child's level of understanding and emotional maturity. Even if you choke on the words at first, it will get easier.

Step 5: No matter what your child asks, don't make them feel ashamed or dirty if they use terminology they have heard – at any age. They will feel relief at being able to say the word out loud in a safe context, which often takes away the appeal of using it elsewhere. Keep in mind that they are opening up to you in the safe context of your discussion and you need to honour that.

It usually helps if you are not afraid to laugh a little. Ask about some colloquial, slang or rude terms your children have heard. This breaks the ice and brings a bit of humour and realness to the situation.

TRY THIS:

After listening to and answering your child's question, you might say, 'Honey, you might have noticed that word you just asked me about is not something you have ever heard me use before, because it is very disrespectful to women [for example]. In our home, we try to use language that shows we care about others.'

Or finish with reassurance: 'I'm so glad you asked me and not someone else. Please come to me any time you hear something or want something explained and we can chat again.'

5. X-rated versions are already flying around the playground (and the smartphone)

It is a natural reaction as a parent to want to protect and shield children from unpleasant or distressing facts. I have found, however, that many parents assume that their children are more unaware than they really are. Each year, in my sexuality development and puberty lessons for pre-teens, I still come across parents who have never even considered talking with their children about their bodies. Parents sometimes think that even at age 11 or 12 their children still don't know anything about changing bodies or sex. Yet most school-aged (and even preschool) children are exposed to media which involves sexualised themes. I remember taking my then 4-year-old son to a little girl's party, and the musical backdrop to pass-the-parcel was hip-hop, sex-infused MTV on the big screen in their lounge. This stayed on for the duration of the party, for 4-year-olds! (I wasn't as good as speaking up then.)

So unless you live in a cave, children know a lot more than you realise, via their peers. The problem is that much of this information will be misinformation. If not acknowledged and discussed, the concerns and anxieties of children about images can become too frightening or difficult for them to deal with.

Parents play a vital part in shaping their child's attitudes around sexualised media messages. The way we talk about our own bodies and relationships will affect what our young people absorb about their meaning. How we view men and women and the roles they play, as well as engaging in open dialogue about sexualised images in magazines, YouTube, games and on billboards, will provide a platform for our children to critically analyse and explore the messages around them. If they don't get it from you they *will* get it somewhere else, which leaves kids vulnerable to unreliable sources, trying to work through the meanings of sex and relationships on their own.

Experts advise that talking about sex and bodies should have begun before a child reaches 8 years old, but don't panic if your child is older and you haven't started yet. You can start now. It's never too late – remember, your children want to hear from you!

TRY THIS:

If it feels overwhelming and you don't know where to start, you might begin with something like, 'When I was growing up I could never talk to my parents about sex or sexuality and I may have brought some of that culture into our home. I know it may seem a bit awkward at first, but I think it is an important topic for us to be able to chat about because I really care about the adult you will become.'

6. Expect each child to be different

Even children in the same family can be very different. Some are very private and like to chat a little bit at a time, while others will chat, loudly, while washing the car in the driveway! Although each child is different, it is of course important that we are careful not to burden children with information for which they might not be ready. We need to adhere to well-known guidelines regarding the appropriate cognitive stages of development of children (see the following chapter for these).

When talking with your child it is important to consider: their age, temperament and stage of development, how secure they are, how you as a family react to particular events, how exposed your child may already have been to particular images, how adequately they can discuss their feelings and emotions on a day-to-day basis, what the influence of their peer group is like and how this group is responding to the issue.

7. The many facets to sex education

In my opinion, the most important part of our conversations with young people is to teach children that there are many layers to relationships. The physical aspect – which schools usually cover and which parents often breathe a sigh of relief over, because 'the sex talk' is done – while important, can often be reduced to a list of 'don'ts', while the key emotional, psychological and social qualities of sexual relationships get left out of discussions. This must be covered, by both mums and dads, if we are to address relationships adequately.

But what if my child or teen doesn't ask anything?

For those children who don't ask, you will need to gauge the appropriate age for discussions and then just begin with little snippets of information. It is important to remember that some children will continue to bring up a topic often, while others will not. For those who do not, I have found that they are mostly still very curious and it is important for you to purposely, yet slowly, bring up and discuss new elements as they get older. I have three children, and each child is completely different in their approach and manner of communication about sexuality, sexualisation and conversations about a pornified world.

Key Messages

- Decide on the three values that are the most important to your family and use them as the foundation for your family discussions.
- Have regular chats about sex and sexuality at each age and stage of your child's life rather than expecting one big chat at the onset of puberty to do the job.
- Parents play a vital part in shaping their child's attitudes around sexualised media messages. The way we talk about our own bodies and relationships will affect what our young people absorb about their meaning.
- Keep conversations and information appropriate to your child's age and level of development to avoid burdening them with material they're not ready for yet.
- Aim to talk about all the aspects of sexuality and relationships, not just the physical side.

CHAPTER 4

Age-appropriate conversations

Many parents view their children and teens as less aware of pop culture messages or about bodies and relationships than they actually are. This often leaves children with a knowledge of something that is confusing or frightening, and which they really need an adult to help them process. Silence on a topic does not mean they don't want to talk to you, it is just that they may be afraid of your reaction, be unsure of how to bring up the subject, or it may not even occur to them that the information they have is inaccurate. After all, if you're 7 and a 15-year-old cousin tells you something, then it *must* be true. Mustn't it?

Part of having good conversations with young people means we need to remember to *listen, listen, listen* and only then talk. Our children need to feel heard, know that their opinions matter and that we aren't just making time to give another lecture. If they know that we respect their opinions and won't laugh at their questions, we will find that they open up and begin to communicate, a little more each time, about some of the topics listed in this book.

Conversations with toddlers and young children

We don't need to have explicit conversations about porn culture with little children. Little ones do not have the maturity or clear understanding of sexualised behaviour. Much of what we teach at this age will be about body safety, the correct terms for body parts and where babies come from. In essence, toddlers and very young children need reassurance and language for appropriate boundaries, more than too many facts. It is also important to help them distinguish fantasy from reality. Young children are still concrete learners, so most things they see will appear true or real until someone points out the opposite.

TRY THIS:

- **Play with your children**

Yes – that's where the firm foundation starts. Play is the work of childhood. It so important that the American Academy of Pediatrics recently released a report[1] on the healing and protective powers of play. The Academy strongly recommends paediatricians 'prescribe' play for children and their parents, because it builds safe, stable and nurturing relationships. It is a vital factor in developing social-emotional competence and learning how to interact with adults and peers. It also promotes language and cognitive development, and enhances brain structure. Even working parents can spend a short time in the evening playing a game of their child's choice, and on weekends visiting a park. Setting aside time to play with your child helps forge bonds and strong foundations for future conversations on the trickier topics. This one-on-one focused time communicates to a child that they matter to you. This is the start of special dates, at each stage of your child's life.

- **Be prepared**

That's more easily written than done, I know! I don't think many of us are ever prepared to hear our children ask their first question about sex. It usually feels too soon and tends to happen when least expected, like when your 5-year-old decides to ask exactly *how* your obviously pregnant neighbour's baby 'got *in* there' – at the precise moment you are out on the driveway, unpacking the groceries from the car and said neighbour comes across to borrow some milk! But even if you weren't prepared the first time a question was asked and you feel like you messed up, you can still say to your child, 'That was a really important question you asked Daddy while we were at the car earlier. I was just busy for a second, but I want to answer you properly. Can we sit and talk about it now/tonight/before bed?' In years to come, your children won't remember the one question you answered badly, they'll remember that they could ask their parents anything.

- **Use picture books**

At both this stage and even into middle primary years, picture books and stories are a fantastic way to introduce new topics. Children learn a great deal through stories, and the quality time with a parent, snuggled up with a book, increases the safe bonding experience. Books can be used as a vehicle for asking further questions and prompting your child to think about others' feelings or behaviours. There are many books available on online safety, body safety and treating others with respect that you can use to start new topics of conversation in your home. Some of my favourites are:

- *No Means No!*, *My Body! What I Say Goes!* and *Some Secrets Should Never Be Kept* by Jayneen Sanders, which explore the idea of body safety and boundaries in a way that is age appropriate for younger readers.
- *Gemma Gets the Jitters* by Katrina Roe, a picture book on childhood anxiety, in which my own tips and advice, for parents, are included.

- *The Internet Is Like a Puddle* by Shona Innes, which introduces younger children to the potential dangers when navigating the internet and teaches online safety techniques.
- *Goodnight Stories for Rebel Girls* by Elena Favilli and Francesca Cavallo, stories about real women of the past and the present who have achieved incredible results, despite all odds.

Conversations with mid- to late-primary–aged children

Talk while 'doing' – plan your accidental conversations, but don't rush them to be finished.
> – Colin Wood, Head of Middle School,
> Pacific Hills School, Australia

At this age our children still need our protection and nurturing as they grow. Protection does not mean sheltering or keeping them away from everything negative (as if we could anyway), but assisting our children to grow up in a space where they are free to discover, explore and find out about their skills, abilities and the world around them. We are helping our children to learn values, form beliefs and make wise choices. Without any clear guidelines or any lesson in critical evaluation of the world around them, children feel unsafe and insecure and end up being blown about by any new fad or trend.

By late primary school, it's no longer just about biology and physical development. That is frankly not enough. We need to have slowly but steadily begun to cover the areas of emotion, connection, commitment, exposure to pornography, peer pressure and more.

TRY THIS:

- **Purposeful conversations**

For this age group, you could begin by asking your children how they feel about the world or about a certain issue you know they have seen or heard about. It can be helpful to let them know what you've noticed. For example, you could say: 'I can see you looking worried/upset/interested in ...' Listen first and then once they have chatted to you, check with them to make sure you've got it correct by rephrasing what you heard them say: 'So what you mean is ...' If you're wrong, they will be quick to tell you. Let children know that you hear what they are feeling.

Between 10 and 12 years old, children should be told by their parents everything that will happen to their bodies as they grow. Children are far more open to discussions about sex and their bodies before they hit puberty. Many will remain open if discussions have happened regularly and seem normal in your family. It can be trickier trying to start conversations about sex and porn culture with a teenager, without earlier conversations throughout their lives. Topics become perceived as inappropriate and embarrassing if they have never been brought up in the home. Although it is *never* too late to start talking!

Additionally, don't worry if topics go off track while talking. Children are processing lots of things at once while they chat with you – the colour of the bus going past, the bad test today, the girl in the park eating a lollipop and the chirping bird in the tree. Children often need to mull over what you have spoken about, or play out the conversation with their Lego later. It is likely they will bring up the topic on another day – usually in the middle of the hairdresser or somewhere equally odd to an adult: 'So, Mum, what do you think of this lady showing her bottom to us in this magazine?' You may also need to purposely revisit the topic in a few weeks or months, to make sure your child understands what you talked about, or to see if they have further questions.

- **Special rituals**

Although I have repeatedly mentioned that sexuality talks should be natural, gradual and occur frequently over the child's life, some parents may still enjoy taking their child or tween away for a weekend as a coming of age or rite of passage ritual, where they can chat in a neutral setting over ice creams or campfires. These aren't meant to be about a one-off big talk; they can be either a designated time for parent–child bonding, or a starting point that will form a foundation for chatting about bigger topics many times over. I know a dad who took his 7-year-old son away on a special camping trip, as a start to their basic conversations on how babies are made. They swam, walked, chose a special takeaway dinner and talked. It felt natural to his son and became a fantastic basis for future chats. In our family, we began speaking with our children about their bodies and body safety from a very young age, yet we took each one on a special trip when they were around 11 or 12, and again in their late teens.

- **Special dates**

Some children love going out for a regular milkshake and chat, or to set up a ritual when they want to discuss something that is concerning them (see more ideas in Conversation #6). A few years ago one of my own children began a ritual, which has turned into a regular thing, where they make us each a cup of tea to drink together. The tea is set out on a small table between two chairs on the deck or brought up to my bedroom. When I get called for tea, I drop everything, because I know my child wants to talk about something meaningful to them.

- **Bedtime rituals**

During lights out, sitting on the edge of the bed or lying next to your child in the dark are often favoured times for deeper topics (this is still a special time in our house). It also works particularly well for first-time conversations with children who don't like to make eye contact, or those who feel worried about blushing or seeing a parent's facial expression.

- **Pick your conversation times wisely**

Driving to sport or kicking a ball outside usually works better than during a favourite computer game, or just before a friend is about to arrive for a playdate.

Conversations with adolescents

I mentioned the importance of resilience studies at the start of the book. The Resilient Youth Australia survey of 78 000 children and teens found a significant drop in resilience between 10 and 15 years of age. The revelation for me was that 15-year-olds are far less likely to feel they have an adult who listens to them or to feel 'very hopeful'. Over 40 per cent of respondents felt that they did not have anyone who knew them very well – that is, who understood how they thought or felt. Almost a quarter said they 'had no one to talk to if they were upset, no one they could trust and no one to depend on'. As to why there is such a drop in confidence towards the mid-teen years, it was found that parents often feel less close to their children during adolescence.

These findings are important because teens requiring autonomy and independence is not the same as them not needing their parents in their lives anymore. They certainly need to be given more responsibility and more freedom as they grow older, but they need us just the same at 14 as they did at 4 – only in different ways. Teens need to feel that at least one parent or carer is trustworthy with big topics. As the parent, if we want to talk about sex and relationships and porn culture, we need to keep working to maintain the relationship with our teens, allow them appropriate freedoms, help them develop their own critical thinking skills and keep their trust.

TRY THIS:

- **Allow expression**

Adolescents need opportunities to express themselves and should be encouraged to discuss their thoughts and feelings about problems that affect their world – even topics you may not agree with them on. The topics they are interested in should not be regarded as trivial. Teens are great thinkers and care deeply about their peers and the world around them. If it is important to your teen, it should be important to you. Critical thinking skills can only develop if teens are given opportunities to voice their opinions and engage in robust debate without being ridiculed or shamed. Debate and discussion about popular culture enables your teen to think about their values and make conscious choices about their lives. Enthusiastically encourage them to look for and research alternative opinions to yours and their own.

- **Listen**

Adolescents place high value on being taken seriously, and feeling accepted and understood. So it is important not to minimise what they tell us as 'just a phase'. Reflective listening is often most effective at this stage and involves repeating back what your teen has told you. It might feel ridiculous the first time you try it, but this actually helps teens to feel heard. For example, your teen might say: 'Mum I am so angry with Jin right now. I can't believe he did that to me.' You might reply with, 'I can tell you are really mad with what Jin did there.' Rather than telling your teen how to fix the issue with Jin, reflective listening encourages them to begin figuring something out on their own (knowing they can ask for advice if they need it). Teens need chances to practise making good decisions to get better at it.

Even if you don't agree with your teen's opinion on something, try to refrain from sounding judgemental of their ideas all the time. You might remind them of your family values and clearly tell them you do not share their view from time to time, but that you are interested in hearing how they came about theirs – and mean it! This further encourages the development of critical thinking – i.e. 'Why do I believe what I believe?' – in both the adults and the teens. Help your teen find their 'voice' by listening and letting them speak, and showing that you are not afraid of your opinions being questioned. I am not talking about how you run the household finances, but in situations where values are established. They know their family values by this stage, but teens need to get to a place where they wrestle with values and make them their own. They will not simply internalise a value because you tell them to.

- **Question**

Adolescents do better with open-ended questions about what they are feeling about a specific topic. If you just say, 'So how do you feel today?' they will often answer, 'Fine,' and not give you much else. Instead try, 'How do you feel about X?' or 'What do you think about Y?' or 'What is it that makes Z your favourite movie?' Some teens also do better when asked what their friends may feel about a certain issue. This can come across in a less threatening or judgemental way, especially if you don't immediately launch into an avalanche of criticism of said friend.

The roller-coaster

Adolescence is the time we often experience our highest highs and lowest lows, and it shapes so much of who we become. It is completely normal for teens' emotions to be quite fluid. They can feel like their world is full of promise in the morning and then crushed by the evening. Teens are often communicating to us via their emotional expressions, rather than words, so we need to learn to look for what they are trying to tell us. They can feel deeply and not know how to express themselves appropriately, especially if they feel disempowered, guilty about something or overwhelmed about their world. When things are rough, ride it out with them, or let them know you are waiting in the wings. Wait for the big emotions to pass before trying to engage in controversial topics (see more on emotions in Conversation #2). Teens need us, but they're also looking for increasing independence. Parents can explain that to earn the privilege of independence, they need to be willing to engage in conversation about new age-related behaviours, such as dating.

A bigger picture

When the world seems dark and confusing to a teen, adults can help by encouraging them to look for a broader perspective and focus on some positive aspects in the world, as well as in their own lives. Teach them, whenever possible, to look for instances and examples of positive behaviour, people doing wonderful things. Teach them to look for the helpers. Teens need to deeply know good to recognise the opposite. This will take practice if they have formed a habit of negativity, but I find that most adolescents will have things they feel passionately about and this passion can be used to spark thoughts about making their world a better, more positive place.

Verbal blocks

Besides communicating via emotional expression, when teens use shrugs or phrases like, 'I dunno?', pause and be patient. This often means, 'I haven't thought about that', or 'Hang on and let me think …' Don't be afraid of the pauses and silences. Teens will often come back and chat about something later, when they feel more relaxed or chatty. You might also say, 'Have a think about X and maybe we can chat about it next week, as I would really like to know your ideas about that.'

Again – be ready!

Be ready for when teens want to open up about something – it often happens unexpectedly. Try to stop what you are doing to properly pay attention, otherwise you may have to wait a while for another chance. Many conversations happen at bedtime or late at night, when teens come in from being out with friends. But don't look like you are waiting in ambush. Perhaps be watching TV or be tidying up the kitchen, and when your teen comes in offer them a warm drink or late-night snack. Many teens begin to open up at this time of the day.

Use your teen's mode of communication: technology

Text them (but don't nag and bombard them) with little snippets of information. For example, before a party, say, 'I know you will be the guy who steps in if a girl is being harassed tonight. Luv ya!' Use emojis and memes just for fun. I went through a stage when I would send my teen son Adele memes (think 'Hello from the other siiiiide!') if he didn't answer an important text. It became a joke between us.

Show and tell

Hug your teenager often, or physically connect with them in a way they feel comfortable with. I have countless stories of teens (both girls and boys) wondering why their parents stopped hugging them, coming to say goodnight at lights out or telling them, 'I love you!' One boy told me forlornly, 'Lately, my parents just distractedly wave goodnight from their place at the TV.' (The importance of touch is discussed in detail in Conversation #1.) Teens need us to be both physically and emotionally present for them. Tell your teen regularly that you find them interesting, that you love their conversations and hearing their ideas – try to do this more than giving instructions and telling them what they are *not* doing all the time. Then, watch them flourish as they feel that what they say matters to you, and they realise that you don't think of them as childish.

When confrontation happens

You are the adult, so you need to try not to take things personally. Know when to back off and cut them some slack, or talk when things have settled down. If there is a lot of confrontation, tell your teen that you would like to really know more about them and understand them better, and you would like to try to learn more about their world. Be honest and tell your teen that you really would like to improve your relationship with them. These types of discussions often work better on neutral territory, such as a coffee shop or a park.

Call out the awkwardness

If you haven't had conversations about bodies, sex or porn before, it often helps to begin to talk about the more important issues of love and heartbreak. Ask teens about their friends' and peer group's habits, and share your own funny, awkward or painful stories from your teen years. This often helps get conversations in matters of the heart started without a teen feeling as though they are being personally interrogated. These discussions lead more naturally into conversations about trust, respect, consent, sex and the damage of porn. New and previously unspoken topics will always feel clunky to start with. Hold firm and it will get easier. If the conversation feels awkward, it can be helpful to simply call out the embarrassment between you. Say something like, 'Gosh, I know we've never spoken about stuff like this before and it feels a bit weird for both of us right now, but I really care about you. I want you to have happy, fulfilling relationships, so I am going to persevere with this from time to time if that's okay?'

Also give your teen permission to talk to a trusted adult mentor about these topics if, after countless attempts, they won't open up to you about it.

Everyday stories

Our own everyday stories are powerful vehicles for awkward topics. Our teens aren't 'dumb' when they make mistakes, they sometimes just lack the life experience we have. They are still building their own stories and will occasionally enjoy hearing about when you have messed up too. They need you to actually verbalise that you are not perfect (because they know it already). If you tell them anecdotes of your own funny, awkward or painful stories from your teen years, they respond well to that. You need to be a little vulnerable, to give them permission to be vulnerable with you. Although, be careful not to force your stories onto your children too often – teens can sniff out a lecture disguised as a 'story'.

Special events

Keep looking for creative ways to connect with your teen. The rituals you had when they were young might still work, or they might change with your child's interests. Perhaps add a coffee after shopping for the season's clothes, go for a hike or to a concert, have a quick milkshake together after sport. You might occasionally be able to incorporate time with your teen into something you do at work, or on a work trip. Something I decided to do as my children became teens (and because I have my own business), was to take one of my children away with me, on occasion, when I travelled overseas to run seminars. My daughter was 13 the first time I took her on my work trip to Africa, and almost 16 on the next visit. We shared rooms wherever I went and explored new sights on weekends. I saw things I never would have if she hadn't been there. And because of the type of personality she has, my daughter was brave enough to attend classes at a local school for a week, while I ran seminars during the day. We both made amazing memories together and had opportunities to bond in unique ways. Now my eldest son has claimed my future trip to Europe for his next turn!

Forewarned

Above all, teens need to be told that even when they eventually mess up (they will, because they are human), no matter what they do, no matter what happens, they can come to you. At any time – day or night. This is not a licence for our teens to plan to do the wrong thing without consequence. But I want to know that my teen will choose to call me first, rather than someone else's mum or even end up in hospital because their fear of my reaction was greater than their knowledge of my unconditional love.

Risky behaviours

Teens generally want to fit in and it can be difficult if they are part of a peer group that engages in risky behaviours. It is important to help our teens to think of ways they can 'save face' in front of their friends, in times they realise a situation is getting out of hand. Give them permission to blame their parents as 'the killjoy' or the nag. Come up with text message codes which they can use to say 'get me out of here'. They also need to know that you won't interrogate them with questions after they've asked for help getting out of a situation. (Too many questions might stop your teen from reaching out to you for help again). Also, help your adrenaline-junkie teen to engage in activities where they can take healthy risks such as rock climbing, martial arts or even speed skating. If you feel as though things are out of control, or you are unsure about how to handle continuously tricky, risky or dangerous teen behaviour, please seek professional help.

If your child doesn't want to talk

I know I keep saying this but … please remember that the following big conversations will happen over your child's early lifetime. They're not meant to be had in one sitting, one week or even one year. There will certainly be periods of time when one or more of your children withdraw and do not want to verbalise their thoughts or activities. In general, but especially in times when kids won't talk to us, we need to watch that we don't overwhelm them by bombarding them with questions, out of our own fears. This often causes them to withdraw further.

I believe, if we look carefully, we will become more aware that our children are always talking with us. Perhaps not in words but with nods, tears, facial expressions, anger or shrugs.

Even our adult conversations aren't always with words. Communicating with our children should happen through gestures, silences, just 'being' with them and, of course, modelling certain behaviours ourselves. Keep in mind that sometimes we don't recognise they are communicating with us, because we don't count the long chatter about the latest video game as 'proper' conversation – while for your child it is. We need to learn to listen to what our child likes to talk about, to earn the right to talk about other topics we want to talk about too.

Additionally, children will have their own way of communicating. Some children talk in fits and spurts – with a huge download once a month at midnight – others chatter away in the car every day. Neither is better or 'right'. The trick is to tune in to your child's way of communicating and try to meet them where they are at.

Overall, if you establish an atmosphere of availability and openness, your children will be more likely to come to you when they have questions.

Key Messages

- When talking with toddlers and little children, bond and communicate through cuddles and play. In conversation concentrate on body safety, the correct terms for body parts and where babies come from.
- Conversations with primary school–aged children should move on from biology to feelings, connections, commitments and peer pressure, etc. You may like to create special rituals that allow your child to become comfortable with these conversations.
- In conversation with teens, help them find their voice and show that you are not afraid of your opinions being questioned. Encourage research and critical thinking.
- Your child is always communicating with you, even if it is not in words.
- Listen to what your child likes to talk about, to earn the right to talk about other topics too.

SECTION 2

15 Conversations

Relationship Intelligence

There are as many kinds of love as there are hearts.

– Leo Tolstoy

As a society we still seem to value brain smarts, better known as IQ, above all else. However, in recent years we've begun to learn more about the importance of Emotional Intelligence (EI).[1] We have come to know that where IQ helps us get a job, it is EI and 'soft skills' that help us keep our jobs – or at least succeed in our vocation. But life isn't just about work, is it? While I'm not suggesting we pull our kids out of school, if you recall the 75-year study on happiness, no one ever got to the end of their lives and wished they had spent more time in the office. Hence, if relationships bring lasting meaning and also help with developing resilience, perhaps it is time we focused more of our attention on teaching children what we might refer to as RI – Relationship Intelligence.

My two RI categories that are important to teach children are knowing you are *love-WORTHY* and knowing how to be *love-ABLE*. Essentially, the former encourages self-respect and the latter develops an 'other-respect'. If we frame our RI conversations in terms of these two categories, it becomes easier for us to formulate our own thoughts and to communicate our family ethics. Making tricky topics part of the Relationship Intelligence dialogue will help discussing them seem a little easier.

Raising both love-WORTHY and love-ABLE children

Teaching children to recognise they are love-WORTHY is about teaching children to understand that they are worthy of love. When people learn this they begin to practise self-compassion and self-care, and possess the courage to speak up when they are not treated with dignity. Teaching children that they need to also be love-ABLE instils in them a recognition of the worth of others: they learn that their choices have an impact on other people, and that others are also deserving of compassion and kindness. Love-ABLE people change their behaviour when they realise that their actions might negatively affect another person. Additionally, they are better equipped to speak out when they see others being mistreated. What adult doesn't want their child to be both cared for and caring toward others?

It's important to find a balance between these two categories, because if we teach our children to be only love-ABLE, they become vulnerable to abuse and exploitation through others' selfishness. And if we teach them to only be love-WORTHY, they are likely to develop self-centred and narcissistic-type thinking.

These two categories can help us respond to our young people's underlying questions, dispel their fears, help them avoid badly scarring each other, stop the cycle of destructive relationship patterns, and improve their ability to develop and maintain a broad range of relationships. Done well, these categories can be used in powerful ways to teach ethics to young people.

Naturally, we need to teach teens and young people about hormones, body development, periods, STIs and pregnancy. But there are countless books on these, so I won't cover the biology here. It goes without saying that teaching all areas of development is important, it's just that this seems to be the area exclusively focused on, to the detriment of love education. Kids can't learn about the importance of respect, emotional connection and love in relationships when they only hear about what goes where and topics based on disaster prevention – how to avoid pregnancy or getting an STI. We have enough bad news stories of groups of teens recording what they think is just biology and putting it on social media. It seems no one ever taught them about the more important stuff of sex and people, that is, the humanity involved in sexual encounters.

We must do better than this. We *can* do better than this. Here are some suggestions to get you started.

RAISING LOVE-WORTHY CHILDREN

Body Safety: 'You are the boss of your body.'

We teach children how to hold a spoon, how to brush their teeth and how to cross the road safely, because these are lessons necessary for nutrition, health and safety. But one of the very first conversations we ought to have with children is about their bodies and body safety. It can seem inconceivable that our child may find themselves in a place that puts them at risk, but the earlier we begin these conversations, the better equipped our children are to speak up to protect themselves – and others, if necessary. They also learn early on that topics about bodies are not off limits at home. What's more, we know that the more confident a child appears to be about speaking up and 'telling', the more this deters potential predators. Equally, they will be more confident to come and speak to us when they stumble across (or are shown) sexual content online (pornography is also used as a grooming tool). Of course, talking about 'stranger danger' is important, but we also need to talk to children about the good touch and bad touch of people immediately around them. Without being overly suspicious of every adult in our child's sphere, we ought to be aware that statistics indicate the majority of abusers are known to the child and the family.

A perpetrator often grooms the family and gains their trust in order to access the child.

Toddlers and children

I realise that parents are often embarrassed to talk to others about their child's curiosity about bodies and private body parts, because they don't always know what is considered 'normal'. Most adults' parents never covered this when they were growing up, so they have nothing to fall back on. So for parents to begin conversations with their little ones about body safety, I start by helping them to understand what constitutes healthy curiosity. I assure parents that children have a natural inquisitiveness about their bodies and about sex, although not in the same way a teen or adult might. Sexual curiosity is part of a child's learning about body and gender, so it is important for parents not to react negatively when they notice these normal childhood behaviours.

Unfortunately, the increased reports of child-on-child sexual abuse means we absolutely must be having body boundary conversations with our young ones. Deviant sexual behaviour was once only displayed when children were victims of sexual abuse themselves, but is now linked with children's exposure to online sexual content. (It is also recognised as a form of child abuse). This issue compounds the culture of awkward silence among parents with genuine questions about their children's curiosity, for fear of their child being labelled deviant. My hope is that this list of what's normal will support parents as they protect their children:

- Babies, toddlers and young children enjoy being naked. Nakedness is not a sexual concept to young children, it is simply enjoying the sensation of air or water on their skin, keeping cool or being able to freely move about without being constricted by clothing. Babies are explorers, because they learn through touch – this is why we baby-proof our homes. They will grab whatever is in reach: their toes, the closest toy or the baby wipes, even the dog's food. Equally, young children will touch, rub and explore their genitals when their nappy comes off at change time, bath time or bedtime. This is completely normal behaviour.

- As children develop language, they begin to ask lots and lots of questions. One of the most common (and sometimes most exhausting) questions is 'Why?': 'Why do birds fly?', 'Why does the vacuum make a noise?' It is obvious, then, that children will have questions about their bodies: 'Why do boys have a penis and girls have a vulva?', 'Why is Mummy different from me?' These questions mean children are trying to work out the difference between what it is to be male and what it is to be female, or why their body looks different in some ways from their best mate's.

- In the same vein, children might go through a stage when they show others their genitals or look with curiosity at someone else's genitals during preschool toilet time. This happens particularly with children under 7, who are close in age and who know each other. This is no different from comparing eye colour or shoe styles they hadn't noticed before. Looking at each other's body parts in a matter-of-fact, curious manner and in mutual agreement is considered normal. In other words, no one is being forced to show their body parts to another child.

- Play is the work of childhood. Children naturally mimic and role play the adults they see (firemen, businesswomen, parents). So occasionally playing doctors and nurses and/or mummies and daddies, by kissing or holding hands with children of a similar age, comes from a place of discovering identities. It is perfectly acceptable, however, for adults to gently talk to children about their private body parts being only for themselves (see the 11 tips on pages 63–67), if the adults don't believe the place, timing and amount of play is suitable. Use distraction and point children to other alternatives.

- Using slang or 'rude' words related to body parts or bodily functions is a normal part of childhood. When I taught early primary students, I lost count of the number of times I heard 'poo' and 'wee' yelled out in class, to the absolute glee of the other students.

- Of course, curiosity about how babies are made, 'Where did I come from?' or 'How did my baby brother get in there?' are also natural questions children have. Some may chat about it in a matter-of-fact way, while others become giggly about discussions around body parts, especially once they come to learn what constitutes 'private' body parts.

It is important, however, that if a parent believes any of these behaviours are becoming excessive (or they happen while your boss is over for dinner), gently redirect your child's attention elsewhere. Also use these as opportunities to talk about body privacy.

Warning signs

Warning signs of possible abuse or exposure to pornographic images recognised by child development experts include:

- Knowledge and use of language that moves beyond body parts and simple curiosity.
- Knowledge and use of language about sex, sexual acts and sexual behaviours that would only be appropriate in an adult relationship. Compulsive preoccupation with masturbation, i.e. the interruption of normal childhood activities to masturbate.
- Compulsively touching their genitals in public, even if asked to stop.

- Compulsive mutual masturbation with another child.
- Forced exposure of others' genitals.
- Forcing other children to play sexual games.
- Rubbing their genitals on other people.
- Regularly trying to touch much younger or older children's or adults' genitals.
- Sexually explicit threats.
- Penetration of toys, children or animals.

Essential body safety conversations to have with your young child

Frank conversations about body parts and safety need to happen early and often, in a relaxed manner. It is not essential to hammer out all of the messages at once. Conversations can happen in little snippets while bathing or dressing your child, before a swimming lesson, or when your child asks a question about your body. There are many opportunities that will present themselves. The trick is for parents to recognise these opportunities and use them as teachable moments.

TRY THIS:

There are essential conversations to have in keeping children safe, as most sexual predators are known to the child and to the family. Predators may use pornography to groom children. In many of my seminars, I use this guide by Jayneen Sanders, child protection expert, advocate and author.[1] She has 10 tips for talking to young children about body boundaries and body safety.

1. Naming body parts
As soon as your child begins to talk, name each body part correctly including the genitals, i.e. penis, vagina, vulva, bottom/buttocks, breasts and nipples. Avoid the use of

pet names to describe the genitals. This way, if a child is touched inappropriately, they can clearly state where they were touched. Explain to your child that their private parts are the parts under their bathing suit. Note: A child's mouth is known as a private zone. (My addition: you don't have to explain the danger of forced oral sex. You simply say, 'You don't shove pencils or food into other people's mouths, or let anyone put anything in your mouth.' This covers everything from choking and food allergies to sexual abuse, without saying so explicitly.)

2. Explain the terms 'private' and 'public'

'Private' means just for you. Talk about a toilet as being a private place but the kitchen, for example, is a public space because it is shared. Relate these terms to both spaces and body parts.

3. No one has the right to touch or ask to see your private parts

Teach your child that no one has the right to touch or ask to see their private parts, and if someone does, they must tell a trusted adult straightaway. Reinforce that they must keep on telling until they are believed. As your child becomes older (3+) help them to identify three to five trusted adults they could tell anything to and they would be believed. These people are part of their Safety Network and at least one person should not be a family member. A Safety Network is a list of safe adults that you have discussed with your child, people they know they can go to if they have any fears or worries.

4. Tell a trusted adult

Teach your child that if someone (i.e. a perpetrator) asks them to touch their own private parts, shows their private parts to the child or shows them images of private parts, that this is wrong, and that they must tell a trusted adult in their Safety Network straightaway. Again, reiterate that they must keep on telling until they are believed. (My addition: adults in turn need to learn to recognise disclosures. These may be verbal or non-verbal, accidental or intentional, partial or complete. Children fear not being believed.[2])

5. Talk about feelings

At the same time as you are discussing inappropriate touch, talk about feelings. Discuss what it feels like to be happy, sad, angry, etc. Encourage your child in daily activities to talk about their feelings, e.g. 'I felt really sad when X pushed me over.' This way your child will be more able to verbalise how they are feeling if someone does touch them inappropriately.

6. Use the terms 'safe' and 'unsafe'

Talk with your child about feeling 'safe' and 'unsafe'. Discuss times when your child might feel 'unsafe', e.g. being pushed down a steep slide, or 'safe', e.g. snuggled up on the couch reading a book with you. It is important children understand the different emotions that come with feeling 'safe' and 'unsafe'.

7. Discuss 'Early Warning Signs'

Discuss your child's Early Warning Signs (EWS) when they feel unsafe. Examples of these could be a racing heart, feeling sick in the tummy, or sweaty palms. Let them come up with some ideas of their own. Tell your child that they must inform you or a person in their Safety Network if any of their Early Warning Signs occur. Reinforce that you will always believe them and that they can tell you anything.

8. Discourage the keeping of secrets

As your child grows, try as much as possible to discourage the keeping of secrets. Talk about 'happy surprises' instead, such as not telling Granny about her surprise birthday party. Compare this with 'unsafe' secrets, such as someone touching their private parts. Make sure your child knows that if someone does ask them to keep an unsafe secret, they must tell someone in their Safety Network straightaway.

9. Teach 'No!' or 'Stop!'

Discuss with your child when it is appropriate for someone to touch their private parts, e.g. a doctor when they are sick (but making sure they know a person in their Safety Network must be in the room). Explain that if someone does touch their private parts (without a Safety Network adult there) that they have the right to say 'No!' or 'Stop!' at any time, and hold out their arm and hand while saying so.

10. Reinforce – being the boss of their own body

Reinforce to your child that they are the 'boss of their body' and they do not have to kiss or hug a person if they don't want to. Explain that we all have a body boundary. This is an invisible space that surrounds our body, and no one can enter another person's body boundary unless they allow it.

I would like to add my own point to this list:

11. Sometimes manners don't matter

We spend a lot of time teaching our children the importance of being polite, saying please and thank you. I agree, manners teach children that others matter too (see more about the importance of manners in Conversation #14), but we need to actively give our children permission to 'forget' their manners at times when they feel uncomfortable or when their bodies tell them that someone (an adult or a child) is in their personal space. Tell your child that when their body responds with EWS that is the time when 'manners don't matter' and they can push someone away, use their loud voice, say 'NO', get away as fast as they can and tell an adult in their Safety Network straightaway.

The power of 'good' touch

We've known for many years about the importance of touch for the healthy physical and psychological growth of infants. Hospitals have even introduced kangaroo care and skin-to-skin contact as part of the care of premature babies, because this has proven to aid physical development. Orphanages enlist the help of volunteers to hold and play with babies, because of the benefits to these children's long-term development.

More recent evidence by Dr Spence, with Oxford University, suggests that smell and touch are linked more closely to the emotional centres of the brain than vision or hearing.[3] A shortage of touch we experience today will have detrimental effects on our health and wellbeing, even leading to psychologically damaging effects. Spence believes that love needs touch to make it real, so even though children may hear that they are loved, they need to physically 'feel' love to truly fulfil the affection they crave. Yet in many situations today, interpersonal touch is actively discouraged, and Spence believes that a generation of children are growing up with 'touch hunger'. I also believe that for children to recognise unhealthy touch, they need to have a firm grasp of what 'good' touch feels like.

Affectionate touch

The love and affection of parents and siblings is the first place that children learn 'good' touch – babies learn to feel safe snuggled into Mum's neck or wrapped in Dad's arms. As children grow from toddlers through to teens, they need to be touched in affectionate ways by their parents. Hugs and touch are even known to reduce stress, so it is essential that we find ways to communicate our love for our children through the types of touch that speak their language. Yet we must stop if they say they don't want to be hugged or cuddled in certain ways, even by Grandma. Some children, particularly those on the autism spectrum, don't like some forms of touch. One man on the spectrum told me, 'I can't stand soft fluttery hugs or strokes. If someone hugs me, it must be firm. I enjoy that.' If you are unsure, ask your child what types of touch feel safe and loving for them.

It is imperative that we don't back off from affectionate touch altogether, just because our child doesn't like hugs. Some ideas for affectionate touch might be a tight side hug, a full-on bear hug, a gentle hand squeeze, head massages at night, bedtime arm tickles, fist bumps, a reassuring squeeze of the upper arm, hair ruffles or rough-and-tumble play.

Rough-and-tumble play

Rough-and-tumble play, for both boys and girls, is a fantastic way for children to learn body boundaries. They learn about the physical power of their own bodies and how to be more gentle with a younger child. They get to see how Dad holds back his full strength when tumbling with their younger sibling. Rough-and-tumble games also lead to an understanding that some children choose not to play or don't enjoy these games, which is okay too. Some kids become overwhelmed by wrestling games quicker than others, and when someone says 'stop' or 'no', this needs to be respected and the game needs to end immediately – even if a child is laughing while saying so. The understanding should be that no one gets mocked or ridiculed for not wanting to play tickling or tumbling games. Children also learn that when someone gets hurt, it is no longer 'fun' for that person, even if you are personally still enjoying the game. They learn to hold back and respect others' physical boundaries.

It is our job as parents to fill our child's touch hunger, but bulldozing through with what we think they need will leave children frustrated and overwhelmed. We need to meet their need for affection in ways that are meaningful and loving *to them*.

Key Messages

- Sexual curiosity is part of a child's learning about body and gender, so it is important for parents not to react negatively when they notice these normal childhood behaviours.
- Frank conversations about body parts and safety need to happen early and often, in a relaxed manner. These are essential conversations to have in keeping children safe from predators.
- As children grow from toddlers through to teens, they need to be touched in affectionate ways by their parents. Hugs and touch are even known to reduce stress, so it is imperative that we find ways to communicate our love for our children through the types of touch that speak their language.
- Teach children that 'sometimes manners don't matter'.

Emotional Intelligence: 'You don't have to be happy all the time.'

For humans to flourish, they do not need to be happy all the time. As mentioned at the start of this book, it is unrealistic to expect that people can, or even should, live in a constant state of happiness. If we habitually push aside complex emotions, we lose the ability to develop skills to deal with the world as it is, rather than what we wish it to be. Living in a state of euphoria is not to be human, and certainly does not lead to a flourishing life.

If we teach children to chase happiness as the ultimate emotion, we teach them to chase after anything – or anyone – to feed this emotion. And we fail to teach them about the richness of life. We fail to raise Emotionally Intelligent adults – those who have the capacity to put aside their need for immediate happiness for a greater good, or for the good of someone else. Naturally, I don't mean children should be exploited or used for the sake of someone else's happiness (see more on this in conversations 7 and 9) but that parenting involves teaching children that all emotions are equally important. In learning about their own emotions, children become better at reading others' emotions too, which leads to compassion and empathy development.

Part of fostering Emotional Intelligence involves teaching children that it's okay to experience and show the full range of emotions, but to express them in healthy ways. We can teach children about the relevance and appropriate expression of all the emotions by helping them name what they might be feeling and identify how their behaviour might stem from an emotional response to a particular situation. Teaching our children about emotion means we don't ignore or try to suppress their emotions; rather, we validate their emotions and then help them to steer their expression in a manner that does not hurt themselves or others. Because no matter what, how we feel is never an excuse to hurt people. In other words, all feelings are okay, but all behaviours in response to those feelings are not.

In addition, teaching delayed gratification is an essential element in helping kids learn about controlling immediate emotions. It might make your child happy to sit in the lounge and play Xbox while the family eats dinner at the table for Grandma's birthday. But as parents we know that their short-term disappointment at not getting their way leads to longer-term wellbeing and learning to think of others too.

Adolescents and big emotions

We know a lot less about the teen brain than we think we do. However, various models suggest that the human brain develops from the back to the front.[1] In other words, the prefrontal cortex (the logical, rational, forward-thinking and planning part of the brain) is the last to develop – by around the mid-20s. Many parents have become familiar with these discussions around the prefrontal cortex, but another area of the brain which changes during puberty is the amygdala.[2] This change particularly affects how teens evaluate and process social contexts, because the amygdala is the emotional part of the brain.[3] It seems that teens and adults use a different part of the brain when they interpret other people's feelings: adults use the rational (and fully developed) prefrontal cortex to read facial expressions, which leads to a more accurate understanding of what someone might be feeling, while adolescents will tap into the limbic system, which includes the amygdala, to interpret emotion.

The amygdala is a self-protection mechanism and is designed to be really sensitive to threat. It runs on gut instinct and impulse. So when teens interpret people's reactions through the lens of the amygdala, they might read anger or aggression as the default response, even when there isn't any. Teens also simply lack enough lived experiences to draw on when dealing with a situation. It is therefore helpful to guide teens to recognise that their big emotions can make it easy to miscommunicate and ruin relationships, even when unintended – but it won't always be like this. Teens are looking to understand themselves, and when they understand this tendency, they become open to the possibility that just because they think someone is disappointed or cranky with them, it doesn't necessarily mean that they actually are. Equally, their emotions can drive teens to do wonderful things too – the first step is for them to recognise this.

Teenagers often manage the big feelings they've held in all day by dumping the uncomfortable ones onto their parents, because it is the safest place for them to sort through these – parents become the buffer. This doesn't mean we need to stand for abuse; rather, we need to talk about alternative ways of expressing emotions, during calmer moments after the heat of the situation has passed.

Additionally, part of the natural process of separating from parents and developing independence leads to some challenging of and arguing about parental ideas. I come from a line of strong, feisty women, so our family debates are always fairly loud and passionate. This is not necessarily a bad thing – if it remains respectful. Our teens need to learn to express their emotions in appropriate ways at home before they become explosive or destructive. Setting argument boundaries can help. Argument boundaries should apply to both the adults and teens and might include: heated debates are okay but should not escalate to yelling and screaming; not using insults or belittling; not bringing up past wrongs; never deteriorate into physical retaliation; permission to go for a walk in the garden or around the block until you feel calmer; agreement that you will talk things through (later or the next day) once everyone has settled down.

This is healthy for everyone involved. Our relationship with our teens is vital in their learning Emotional Intelligence, so we need to model healthy ways of expressing strong emotions, and apologising when we have gone wrong. Kids learn that to be human is to make mistakes. Not being too proud to apologise and make amends for hurt caused is a vital life skill.

In talking with teens, I encourage them to speak up if they are worried, and ask the person what they are thinking, which can save heartache. I also point out that emotions often run wild when we are tired, so it's important to get good sleep and refrain from emotionally charged online conversations, especially at night. In addition, teens need to be made aware that alcohol hijacks an already underdeveloped brain. This combination leads to poorer self-awareness and decision-making, and a greater likelihood of misreading others' feelings and reactions. Aspects that their brains are already struggling to figure out. We see far too many heartbreaking teen stories in the media which involve alcohol-fuelled in-the-moment emotional decisions (see more on alcohol in Conversation #10).

Overall, 'emotion awareness' is a good habit for teens to develop, and will become a powerful tool in developing Emotional Intelligence.

More than glad, sad and mad

When I talk to children and teens I often chat about the less-acknowledged emotions. It is important for children to dig down underneath their emotional expression and work out where the emotion is coming from. Don't assume you know exactly how to respond to a child's emotion. You may incorrectly assume that your child needs a hug, when he actually just needs to have someone listen and hear him. Ask your child what they need from you to feel supported or heard – some children just need their emotion to be named or acknowledged.

Anxiety is an example of a less-talked-about feeling. I tell young people that a little bit of fear is important – it is your body's very clever way of keeping you safe. For example, you are afraid of walking in the African bush alone, as a lion may jump out and choose you for his dinner. Or your stress about failing an exam is what moves your butt from the couch in front of the Xbox and into the study to your books. Yet too much fear will cause you to avoid mildly difficult situations, even pleasant situations, and can also paralyse you. That is not healthy fear. So we need to help kids become the boss of their fear.

Teaching children to manage and respond appropriately to strong emotions is difficult and takes time. As different emotions are experienced in varying degrees, depending on the circumstances, using synonyms for their emotions can be helpful in learning to express nuanced feelings. Be patient and don't expect more from a child than you can manage yourself.

TRY THIS:

- 'Use your words to express your feelings. Don't bottle them up. Don't shove them down. Feelings are what make us human. Emotion is what it means to be alive.'
- 'What do you need from me to feel supported in this situation?'
- 'If you were talking to a friend, what advice would you give him/her about this problem?' (This concept

helps children practise self-compassion and look at the problem from another angle.)

- 'When you feel overwhelmed, it's often helpful to take some deep breaths, then find something quietly distracting to do until you feel like you are ready to move on or talk about it.' Brainstorm with your child and come up with age-appropriate and healthy activities she can engage in when facing strong emotions. The more ideas the better, e.g. listening to music, painting, squeezing a stress ball, going for a jog, or chewing gum.

Emotion-specific statements

- **Happiness:** 'I can tell by your reaction that this makes you really happy.' 'What is it that makes you happy about this issue?' 'Should we celebrate this?' 'How can you tell when someone is really happy?'
- **Sadness:** 'I am sorry, I can tell that something hurt you.' 'Would you like to tell me about what made you sad/ upset in this situation?' 'Is there anything you would like me to do?' 'Do you need me to help you speak with someone?' 'I heard that Simon's grandma died. What do you think you might like to say to him at school tomorrow?'
- **Anger:** Responses to anger outbursts are usually best left until the emotion has settled down or when the situation is not explosive. Then try, 'I can tell that this made you angry.' 'You sounded angry about that.' 'Is there another way you could channel your anger in future, in a healthier way/in a way that doesn't hurt your sister?' 'It's okay to feel angry or hurt about something, but it is not okay to hurt someone else in your anger.' 'I can see you were angry earlier, but I wonder if there is something else that you are feeling underneath?' 'Anger is sometimes the first thing that comes out, but there is

sometimes another emotion bubbling underneath. What happened just before you began to feel the anger rising?'

- **Disgust:** 'I can tell you are disgusted by that.' 'Is there something I can help you with, to reduce your feeling of disgust?' 'Is there something we could do to respond to the situation that disgusts you?'

- **Fear/worry/stress:** 'Fear isn't a "bad emotion", it's your body's way of keeping you safe, but if it paralyses you, we need to find a way for you to process your fear in a healthier way.' 'What is it that makes you worried about this? Could we break up the task into smaller, more manageable chunks that are less overwhelming?' 'When you are stressed, you react in a way that sometimes hurts the others around you. Can we think of ways you could express your anxiety that will help you, but doesn't hurt others?' 'When Sally is worried about her test, what do you think might be helpful to say/do for her?'

- **Guilt:** 'A sense of guilt can come about when we know we haven't done something honest or kind. It's like when our conscience tells us that taking the chocolate from the shop, or teasing the boy at school, was wrong.' 'If we squash this feeling too often, we can stop our bodies from telling us when something is right or wrong.' 'There are also times when your mind tricks you into thinking you should feel guilty, but something wasn't actually your fault. Can you think of times when this could happen?'

- **Love:** 'Love can be a beautiful feeling, but sometimes it can be a little scary too.' 'What tells you that I love you?' 'How might we show your sister that we love her?' 'There are so many ways to express love, I know it can be confusing, but let's chat about some of them.' (See more on romance and relationships in conversations 3, 9 and 11.)

- **Excitement:** 'I can tell you are really excited about that.' 'What brings you excitement in your life?'

'I know you love excitement. What are some safe ways of experiencing excitement?' 'Do you think sometimes a person's excitement for something might bring harm to someone else who doesn't find it exciting?'

- **Courage:** 'What do you think it looks like for someone to be quietly brave?' 'What does open bravery look like?'

Use these examples to think of other emotions and statements that might be helpful for your child.

The power of pets

If you are able, get a family pet. The unconditional love of a pet is a powerful way for children to experience and express emotions, not to mention develop a sense of responsibility. Many organisations and some schools incorporate therapy dogs into their wellness days, because they recognise the power of animals in people's lives. I know, I know – Mum or Dad might end up nagging the kids to feed the animals. But the overall benefits of having a pet to care for, love and talk to are immeasurable.

Talking to girls about their emotions

It seems we have been better at allowing girls to express their emotions or to be more emotional than boys. Although we do need to be watchful that we don't indirectly imply that girls' expression of emotion makes them weaker than boys. We also need to look for opportunities to talk to girls about strength emotions and character traits that are more traditionally used for boys, like bravery and courage. Moreover, when they are deeply moved by something, they need to know that they can channel their emotions to drive change in the world around them.

On friendships

Girlhood relationships are so important, yet they can be both wonderful and terrible in the same week. As a girl moves through the school years, friendships can become intense. During my 10 years as a school counsellor, I noticed that there was a period when girls' negative friendship issues ramped up, starting around 9 years and intensifying further between 13 and 15 years of age, more so than boys at this stage. What's happening around this time is girls are changing from being little girls, reliant on parents and friendships they've had for years, to becoming more independent. They're developing into young women and their likes, tastes and interests begin to change. They want to explore the possibilities of new friendships and find out about new people and new activities. This often leads to hurt when one girl is not ready for another friend to expand the friendship circle. I tell girls that changes in friendships are a normal part of growing up – although never an excuse for meanness.

Girls need to know that arguments or disagreements are normal and okay, but they need to remain respectful. Modelling apologies at home is a good start (this goes for boys too, of course). When you're a young person (actually, make that any age), friendship fallouts hurt, but children need to know that arguing doesn't have to be the end of the world – or the friendship. Developmentally, some squabbling is vital because it helps us learn conflict resolution.

When inevitable conflict arises, girls can often get caught in a 'rumination loop' – they replay the scene over and over in their minds, like a song stuck on repeat, which makes the situation feel catastrophic. So, because you know your daughter's brain is still learning how to interpret some responses, and if you suspect she may be misinterpreting a friend's words or signals, ask her to look for evidence to support her interpretation. Whether she finds the evidence or not, suggest your daughter talk to her friend privately and in person – without an audience. Teach her to be assertive, rather than aggressive in her communication, and to plan beforehand what she would like to say. Help her start with

'I' words, which encourage girls to own their feelings and their experiences. She could say, 'I felt let down when you ...' or 'I'm sorry. Can we fix this and be friends again?'

Although painful, not all relationships are meant to continue forever. Acknowledge the hurt in your child and reassure her there are many new, interesting people she will meet throughout her life.

I encourage parents in this period to ensure that their daughter has friends they don't see every day. Seeing people outside of their day-to-day social circle is a way to relieve the pressure. This might mean occasionally hanging out with a neighbour, someone they know from their sporting team or a family friend's child. They can provide a more relaxed friendship – and back-up when things aren't going well. It also helps the child to realise they are not alone. When girls have opportunities to be involved with others who have similar interests to them, they often find their tribe.

Adults can also help girls to realistically recognise what it means to be a friend, as well as what they are looking for in a friend. Brainstorm by using sentence starters like, 'A good friend is a person who ...' This helps girls to recognise what they value in others, but also what a toxic relationship might look like.

Navigating toxic 'friendships'

Most girls will experience the pain of interacting with a toxic 'friend' or 'friends' during their school years. Boys do too, but in different forms. Psychologists call this type of interaction 'relational aggression' and it serves to damage a person's sense of social place. For example, a girl (or group of girls) appears to be friendly but uses passive-aggressive strategies, like gossip, belittling (explained away as 'just joking'), exclusion from parties, online conversations, or even seating arrangements on the bus, as forms of emotional bullying. (Boys experiences can involve exclusion from playground activities, social events or online gaming groups, or they could become the target of continuous unhealthy banter.) This can be a very confusing time in the tween and teen years, and leads to feelings of shame and loneliness.

The problem is that, compared with boys, many girls are taught from a very early age that anger is always bad. So when girls are faced with the social pressure to be good at all costs, it makes it very difficult for them to stop and say, 'Hang on, the way you're treating me makes me feel angry and hurt. I'm not going to allow you to treat me that way any longer!' If girls don't have healthy ways of expressing their anger and hurt to someone, they will often internalise these emotions. This presents in a number of unhealthy ways, like self-harm, anxiety, eating disorders, self-loathing and more.

Adults can support girls by teaching them how to channel their anger at injustice effectively, without resorting to physical or verbal expressions that just escalate the hostility. This can be done through role playing or modelling assertive communication and respectful anger strategies. It can also be done by giving girls permission to draw boundaries and walk away from a toxic relationship for the sake of self-preservation.

Adults need to be available as the safe place – the sounding board – for girls to vent or cry when they are hurting and want to process a problem. Adults may not be able to solve the problem or change the toxic person's behaviour at this time, but shouldn't underestimate the power of listening and being available to their hurting daughters. Obviously there will be times when things might escalate and need to be taken to the school for further intervention. However, in many circumstances, helping girls to develop skills for dealing with mean people also provides them with a life skill and teaches them how not to treat others in the same way. It is at times like this that I strongly advise parents to help their daughter to draw strength from the other networks I mentioned above. Then, when excluded from a party, a parent can arrange for their daughter to hang out with another girl in her broader network. It doesn't solve the party problem, but does help your daughter not to feel isolated and alone on the party night.

Your daughter will make friendship mistakes, but in using the skills above and explicitly teaching your daughter compassion, kindness and empathy, you will help her not to become a toxic person herself.

About boys

Teach your daughter about friendships with boys and that not all boys are *gross* or *weird*. Talk about brothers, male cousins or family friends, to give examples of how boys and men also have hopes and dreams, just like they do. Emphasise that she should not toy with anyone's emotions, because boys feel deeply and can be very hurt by girls also.

As with toxic friends, girls need skills to recognise and walk away from toxic males or romantic partners (see more in Conversation #7 on respect).

Dads, hug your daughters often! Even when she is a teen. If she absolutely hates it, find a different way to communicate your love and physical affection. It must be something that she likes and on her terms. It may be sitting together on the couch, squeezing her hand, or kissing her forehead goodnight. Don't ever give up showing her you love her. You must be a safe place for her. She will learn through you not to settle for less from men.

Watch the language we use with girls

Never ever use the phrase, 'He is mean to you because he likes you'. This saying makes hurting an acceptable form of gaining attention or, worse, a meaningful form of communicating affection. This sets children up for vulnerability to abuse. Talk about the importance of your daughter's voice and of her feelings being respected by the men and boys around her.

On female strength

An Australian survey of more than 1700 girls aged 10 to 17 discovered 98 per cent believed they were treated unequally to boys, particularly in sport, the media, at school and at home.[4] Girls need not to just hear they have emotions or character traits similar to their brothers, they need to have this demonstrated to them. Girls need to be given opportunities to be strong and brave, rather than just pretty and sweet. This can be explored through play, through conversations, or through the tasks they're allowed to perform at home and at school. For example, girls ought to be allowed to use a drill and not just the broom when helping parents around the house. Girls need to be allowed to voice a strong opinion and say no when they disagree with someone's behaviour. Schools and families need to show more support for Australian women's sporting teams and achievements, the same way they do for men's teams. Strong female leaders need to be invited to speak and inspire both boys and girls at school assemblies and cultural heritage days.

Talking to boys about their emotions

On toxic masculinity and challenges to boys' emotional expression

The term 'toxic masculinity' has gained a lot of attention of late. It is often misunderstood or misinterpreted. I want to stress that I don't mean to insult or hurt anyone and will begin by clarifying a little first. Two of my three children are boys. My sons and my husband, and so many of their friends, are not 'toxic' simply because they are male. Just as in the section for girls on 'toxic friendships' where it ought to be obvious that friendship itself isn't toxic, nor are all friends toxic, 'toxic masculinity' does not imply that masculinity, all men or maleness are bad.

There are so many versions of masculinity, and 'toxic masculinity' describes a limiting culture of masculinity that is toxic *to* men. A 'masculinity' which limits the emotional range allowable to men and boys primarily to expressions of anger. One which expects men to seek to be dominating, through force, fear or manipulation. (Dominating is not the same as being a strong leader. There are many men who are inspiring leaders, without having to dominate and suppress others.)

Part of the toxic culture for young men is that many will have Friday night drinking buddies to laugh and joke with, but no one to actually talk to about how they feel when life is tough. This social isolation is literally killing them. Research now tells us that young men who embrace the toxic messages about what it means to be a man are more likely to struggle with depression,[5] under-report self-harm,[6] disregard their health[7] and display risky behaviours like binge drinking.[8]

Although we are getting better at encouraging boys to express their emotions in more healthy ways, emotional development still often gets squashed around adolescence, mostly due to the way we celebrate masculinity at the expense of emotional and social development. Toxic masculinity often happens when good dads and elders are absent, and a boy's peer group becomes the main source of information and perceived wisdom. Add to this the plethora of poor male sports star and celebrity behaviour, which is often excused as 'just what men do'.

Recognising messages that are toxic to our boys' development, is the first step towards a healthy and strong masculinity characterised by rationality, integrity, health, compassion and resisting poor social pressure.

Some examples of toxic masculinity

Unhealthy boy banter

Fun, teasing and a little sarcasm are normal parts of friendship. There's nothing wrong with these. The problem is when banter becomes the only way that boys know how to relate to one another. Constant banter often leads to boys taking things too far and hurting their mates through regular mockery and sarcasm. When everything needs to be a joke, even in one-on-one settings, this results in a habit of avoiding emotional engagement or going deeper in relationships. Boys tell me that they want to be more emotional with their mates and talk about life issues, but they are afraid. They fear being shamed by being called a 'pussy', told to 'man up', to 'stop being a girl' or that they are 'gay'. They are also afraid of how it will feel when they begin to share. A 16-year-old boy told me that 'sharing your heart can sometimes hurt.' Having an adult to verbalise his emotions with provides a boy with opportunities to use words, rather than just actions, to express what he is feeling. Parents might gently call out unhealthy banter by saying, 'It's really fun to have a laugh with your mates but be careful that you don't take your jokes too far. Your mates won't tell you if you have hurt them, but maybe just hold back from always having the last word?' (See the section on developing emotional expression on pages 90–92.)

'Fuck boys'

Perhaps not something new to this generation, but this is the group known by many teens currently as 'F-boys' or 'fuck boys'. This group is known for their dangerous normalisation of sexual objectification, entitlement and harassment of girls. A toxic environment ensues when power, manipulation, charm and entitlement are combined with the inability to express emotion and vulnerability. In a group setting this is often shown through excessive drinking, hooking up, partying and pressuring girls for nude photos. It is the default safety net that some boys fall into, which develops out of social and emotional insecurity. Vulnerable girls who already struggle with their sense of worth can be drawn in by the attention of F-boys, without realising how much they can hurt them. Vulnerable boys might be drawn into a group of F-boys, because they appear confident and cool and are getting some girls' attention. Teens need strong men and women, as healthy role models, who will call out this culture as broken, and point out how destructive it is to both men and women. The destructive nature of this group might be obvious to adults but to many teens it is a powerful message when we speak up about it.

Boys and anger

Anger is especially important to highlight here, as it is still the more socially acceptable manner in which boys express other emotions, such as sadness, fear or pain. If we teach boys to look underneath the anger they have long been encouraged to express, they will begin to recognise that it was sometimes never anger in the first place. Angry, aggressive men were once little boys, taught that power and dominance are the key ingredients to 'success'. And then when these boys were bullied, hurt or felt weak, they internalised a sense of shame.

Shame leads to boys vowing to themselves that they will never allow anyone to make them feel that way again. So these boys become young men who strive to do whatever it takes to be at the top of the power chain; in sport, work, activities and relationships. If they make it, they continue to laud it over others through emotional, physical or psychological means, all the while hiding their insecurities. If they don't 'make it', their shame is magnified. Either way these men can still silently struggle with inner demons, self-doubt and various mental health issues. All boys need to learn healthy ways (rather than through displays of anger) to deal with, talk about and channel their emotions, so that they grow into emotionally well-rounded men. I believe this is vital if we are to effectively combat domestic violence.

The 'dumb dad' narrative

Somehow we moved directly from books and movies showing emotionally detached dads, served by women and children, doing all the brave, cool or 'important' jobs and tasks, to the dumb dad character. That is, dads in front of a TV screen, with beers and big bellies, hardly able to string a few intelligent words together, and who are still emotionally detached. And mothers of sons, please don't refer to your husband as 'the other boy' in the house. It is belittling and sends a message to your sons that their dad hasn't grown up. Our boys need to see involved, emotionally confident dads celebrated in our homes and in the media. Point out stories with great dads who don't need alcohol to have fun, have a good work ethic, share the household chores, cook great meals, play with and cuddle their children, and are affectionate towards their wives and partners.

Withdrawal

Many young adult men and fathers I speak to tell me that they deeply crave close male friendships, other men they can confide in and share their fears, aspirations, sadness and joys. Yet only a few seem to have this. Why? Something happens where men become conditioned to adopt tough stoicism over warm emotional connection. Little boys, like their sisters, seek out strong, tactile, compassionate, remorseful, loyal, loving, gentle, kind and passionate friends. We need men who recognise this to model to boys that male sharing of emotion is okay, even vital, to their overall health. It's not that I expect men to still act like boys – research backs my anecdotal evidence that many men are extremely lonely. Suicide rates among men yell out that something isn't working, and we need to change it!

Processing romantic rejection

Without learning appropriate expressions for a strong emotion or when faced with rejection, boys often fall back on the only socially acceptable way for men to express pain: aggression. Research tells us that men who are stressed because they see themselves as less masculine can be prone to more violent behaviour.[9] Experiencing a heartbreak can lead to teen males' belief that their social identity is threatened, and they may compensate with over-demonstrating their masculinity, through unhealthy stereotypical ways like increasing their level of banter, stepping up displays of emotional toughness, hooking up with girls at parties or, worse still, by lashing out in vengeful ways at their ex-partner.

We can teach boys to cope with inevitable rejection, be it in sporting, academic, friendship or romantic realms, in healthy ways. This can be done through non-judgemental, supportive dialogue. In addition, secure family attachments in childhood lead to a decrease in the likelihood of violence against a romantic partner later in life.

On the language we use with boys

We need to watch our own language about boys at home, in the classroom, on the sporting field, or while watching a movie. We might begin by examining popular phrases we've taken as the norm.

'Man up' and 'Be a man' – Yes, there are certainly times in a young man's life when he needs to begin taking responsibility for his decisions and actions. We don't want men overly dependent on their parents at 25. However, telling a boy to 'man up' has traditionally been used to shame a boy or male teen when he cries or displays what is considered to be too much emotion. We all sometimes need to 'suck it up' if we are trying to simply avoid doing a task we don't want to do, but we need to be careful that this phrase is not used to suppress our sons' emotions. We ought to call out times when people use this phrase to imply displaying emotion as a weakness.

'You throw like a girl' and 'Cry like a girl' – If we think about it, we've never heard a coach say, 'Wow, you threw like a girl!'

where he meant, 'Wow – what a fantastic throw! Great job!' 'Like a girl' is a term that is used as an insult. It's often said between boys and implies that the way he performs an action is done poorly, and that, by default, girls aren't very good at said activity. It implies weakness and that displays of emotion aren't for men. It sends the indirect message that girls are over-emotional and boys ought not to be. The term is demeaning and disrespectful.

'Boys will be boys' – Unfortunately, this term is also often used to excuse little boys when they physically or emotionally hurt each other or hurt girls, or exhibit bad behaviour. Many boys are more fidgety and physically active than girls at younger ages. Some of this is partly due to the different rates and stages at which boys and girls develop. So, when we see a backlash against the term 'boys will be boys' it's not denying some of their different rates of development, it's a reaction to the way the term has been used to excuse poor behaviour.

On strength

What parent does not want their son to grow up into a man with strength of character? We need to counter what they hear about strength through poor sports role models and the media. In the media a man is often called strong when he displays physical strength, brashness, bravado or dominates others, but we need to reframe compassion, standing up for others and kindness as powerful, and gentleness as a strength. Even anger, when aimed at injustice, is a sign of good character. Through modelling, we can teach both little boys and big teens that to stand up for the weak is courageous. Then follow this by actively noticing when our sons are gentle with young children, kind to girls, loving with Mum, respectful to the elderly, or protective of animals. Adults should also model apologising and demonstrate that saying sorry when you are wrong or have hurt someone is a strong character trait.

Boys are also beautiful

I have seen the opposite of toxic culture in my own family and in the teen boys I work with. It is evident in beautiful displays of 'brotherhood' or 'mateship': boys loving and caring for their mates in powerful ways. When boys refer to their mates, in healthy friendships, as 'my bros', this refers to mates who have your back, don't 'dob each other in', don't try to hit on your romantic partner, who you can be yourself with and have healthy fun with. They are like family and what we wish for all our sons to have.

This account was written by a mum of three boys and submitted to Exploring Teens, an online community.[10] It brings a story of hope, something we need to focus on more.

I just want to say how fabulous teenage boys can be.

One of my sons (year 12) had a rough morning a month back with his anxiety running wild. We arrived at school after a pretty epic meltdown in the middle of the trip that left me as rattled and anxious as it did him. Together, we weren't a pretty sight.

After calming down and regaining some level of composure, I asked him what he wanted to do. Should we wait in the car a while longer or did he want me to just drop him off in the usual 'kiss and drop' location?

He said he was happy to be dropped off (by this time the bell had gone and there weren't many around). As we approached the area, we saw one of his best friends just standing there. I baulked and said to my son, 'What do you want me to do? Should we wait back here till he's gone?'

'No,' my son said, 'don't worry, go ahead, I'll deal with it.'

So I slowly drove into the drop-off area and let him out. I pulled away from the kerb, terrified for the embarrassment he might feel, and just happened to glance in my rear-view mirror.

What I saw stole my heart and left me in a mess of tears again
… There was my 6-foot-plus son being hugged in a huge,
warm and unrestrained embrace by his 6-foot-plus friend.
I truly love my boys and their friends!

How can adults break the emotion-stunting pattern and grow boys who are more comfortable with emotion as a character strength?

Developing emotional expression

Boys need to hear that a 'real man' is a 'good man', and a 'good man' is emotionally aware, that emotional expression, or displays of grief or vulnerability, require courage – not weakness – and this outstrips what is needed to bully or dominate others. They need to know that care and comfort and emotional connection take self-reflection and confidence. Although when they feel self-doubt, this is part of being human too, and it is okay to communicate that they don't know it all. That they are still learning about themselves and others.

- Let your son cry. Tell him it's okay to cry, to feel deeply moved, to express sadness.
- Dads, let your son see you cry and express pain, loss or sadness in appropriate ways.
- Tell your son that it sometimes feels painful to be vulnerable, to share your fears or worries, and that's normal.
- Tell your son how beautiful you think his heart is, and what you've noticed him do.
- Tell your son about a non-stereotypically male character trait you admire in him, such as kindness.
- Encourage your son to express his deep emotion, his loves and his pain openly, especially into his teen years – and help him practise using new nouns and adjectives to describe these.

- Specifically, help your son to understand, from a young age, that rejection is a part of life and is not a reflection of his manliness or a statement on his self-worth. Help him find healthy ways to move forward and continue to talk to someone about his pain.
- Teach your teen son that it is normal to have a deep love for close male mates.
- Tell your son he has the capacity for reason, empathy and choice.
- Tell your son that hitting or pinching a girl is never a way of telling her he likes her. Teach him how to properly communicate affection: with kind words and gestures.
- Teach your son that anger is never an excuse to hurt others. Teach him about self-control – it is not 'manly' to be cruel.
- Teach your son to channel his anger into causes that fight injustice.
- Hug your son often, even when he is a teen. If he absolutely hates it, find a different way to communicate your love and physical affection. It must be something that he likes. It may be sitting together on the couch or a side hug. Don't ever give up showing him you love him.
- Dads and male carers can also model what it looks like to have and be a close mate to other men. (Perhaps this is something you need to pursue for yourself?)

Talking about the footy is fun, but we need to make times when we ask some of the deeper questions of life. There are many resources that can support parents and sons in developing deeper conversations. A fantastic example is The ManMade Toolbox by Andrew Lines.[11] It is a set of 87 cards divided into 6 suits: *My Stuff, Body Stuff, Head Stuff, Relationship Stuff, Big Stuff, Future Stuff.* It helps men and boys (from age 13) tell their story through language and creating conversations.

For both boys and girls – on emotion and social media culture

Communicating through a screen can be a powerful form of connection which can and does enhance healthy friendships. However, online communication can also lead to toxic interactions, such as bullying, exclusion, pressuring each other to send or ask for nudes, sharing of pornography (see more on porn culture in conversations 9, 10 and 13), posting pictures of girls for ratings, or inappropriate private messaging conversations. Much of this can seem more transactional than real (i.e. to gain more likes and comments as a form of social status), and often chips away at healthy social and emotional development.

Girls tend to use social media in different ways from boys. One study found that this time scrolling through the rabbit warren of social media can lead to additional opportunities for girls to feel left out.[12] Almost half of the girls surveyed said they feel excluded and lonely when they see their friends getting together without them. Of course girls have always felt this way, it's just that social media shows (in real time) when girls are excluded from an event. There is no mental break from it. Photos, videos and messages can encourage both poor choices and great choices, depending upon whether we address them or not. Consistently poor choices online need to be met with consequences.

It is vital that we:

- Talk about social media messages that are unkind, dangerous or which normalise toxic culture (such as sexualisation, objectification, body dissatisfaction).
- Talk to girls about the sadness, frustration and hurt that they can cause others online when one person is left out of a group chat or online interaction. Explain how this is the same as being muscled to the outside of a circle of girls chatting, where you can overhear and

see everything, but you are meaningfully excluded from taking part.

- Talk about online sexual bullying being a form of sexual harassment.

Adults must model, to both boys and girls, that every one of their emotions is equally valid. Also, that it is important to express their emotions, but to steer expressions in ways that are both healthy and safe to others and to themselves. Childhood is the time when there is great potential to unlock social-emotional abilities, which will become habits for life.

Key Messages

- It's helpful to guide teens to recognise that their big emotions can make it easy to miscommunicate and ruin relationships, even when unintended.
- Model healthy ways of expressing strong emotions and apologising when we have gone wrong. Kids learn that to be human is to make mistakes. Not being too proud to apologise and make amends for hurt caused is a vital life skill.
- Encourage both girls and boys that all emotions are valuable and help them to steer their expressions in a manner that does not hurt themselves or others.
- Seeing people outside of a child's day-to-day friendships can provide support in difficult times and reassurance that your child is not alone.
- Changes in friendship are a normal part of growing up – although never an excuse for meanness.

Love Education: 'Love is a beautiful thing. Yes, break-ups are hard.'

I find it incredible that young people need a licensed driver to sit beside them for an entire year before they take to the roads on their own, yet we do very little to prepare them for what is possibly the most important aspect of their lives: an intimate romantic relationship. Adults' lack of modelling and conversations about love, romance and relationships creates a gaping hole in young people's lives. When we fail to adequately support young people in any area, this creates destructive ripple effects throughout their adult lives. We know that a hole always needs to be filled, so young people turn to popular culture for answers.

Authors of a Harvard study raise the alarm:[1]

The harm is not simply daily exposure to misogynistic songs, pornography, and other debased images of sex – serious as that harm is. Many forms of entertainment and media also spawn all kinds of misconceptions and reinforce deeply ingrained cultural myths about romantic love: that love, for example,

is an intoxication or an obsessive attraction; that 'real love'
is clear, unmistakable, and undeniable; that love happens
suddenly and is forever, which means that you shouldn't give
up on it even if it means that you are degraded or shamed.
Media images of love, in part because we are not taught to
view them as aberrant, may be more harmful than media
images of violence.

The good news is that, because many adults don't seem to be engaging young people in meaningful conversations about romance, love and mature relationships, the only way from here is up.

How do we help young people navigate romantic relationships and heartbreak?

We all crave love and connection. As adults, we remember what it was like to long to matter to someone special in our teen years. So, as teens grow up and become independent of their parents and begin to move away from their family, desiring to be intimate emotionally and physically with someone is natural. Exploring romantic relationships forms part of healthy communication, identity and emotional skill development. It is something we need to keep in mind – even celebrate.

Don't be afraid if you don't have all the answers. Kids and teens don't expect you to know everything. What they value is having someone who is unafraid to have frank, open conversations. Adult life experience brings with it stories and wisdom that can be shared, explored and reflected upon with young people.

Sometimes adults can feel as though their own history of pain and broken relationships doesn't give them the right to talk with teens. On the contrary, reflecting on past relationships highlights human issues such as hurt, vulnerability, hopes, misconceptions, fears or joys. It brings lived experience to the conversation. All of this both enriches your relationship with young people, and helps them develop skills in their own romantic relationships.

A quick word of caution: Before sharing personal stories, adults need to think carefully about why they are sharing them. Ask yourself:

- 'Is my story something I need to process with an adult before deciding what to share with my child?'
- 'What is the point of my story?
- 'What do I hope my child will learn from it?'
- 'How will this help teens think through a decision?'
- 'Is what I am sharing age appropriate?'
- 'Will this story be beneficial to my children, or will it become an unhelpful burden for them?'

Once you are confident that what you are sharing will help a young person grow in their relationships, there are a number of topics you can explore together.

The best way to begin the topic of romantic relationships is to start small. Begin by asking what their extended peer group is doing and what your child thinks about the behaviours or relationships of those around them. If this is too close to home for some teens, try using media stories and movies as a starting point: these are less interrogative and give a window into your child's thoughts and struggles. Look for positive stories and great real-life examples to chat about. This will help your children to discover not only what to avoid, but also to focus on the positive goals and dreams they are aiming for in relationships. The more conversations you have, the easier the discussions become and the less likely your child will be to get into trouble further down the track.

Build a culture of sharing

Encourage close sharing by talking to teens regularly about a range of topics well before the first romantic interests surface, so that chatting about relationships doesn't come suddenly and seem forced.

Discuss different forms of love and attraction

More than discussions on sex and porn, talk about the wonder of love and romance. Your teens are interested in this, a great deal. Chat about:

- How real love takes time and leads to flourishing relationships.
- Falling in love and what it feels like to be newly in love. That it is often gloriously heady and breath-taking. Talk about your own first love experience.
- Why and how romantic relationships can be deeply meaningful and gratifying.
- The differences between mature love and other forms of intense attraction, i.e. the differences and combinations of liking, attraction, infatuation, lust, passion and love – how they are not the same thing.
- How there is no fear in love!
- Signs that might identify healthy and unhealthy relationships. And how a healthy relationship should make us better people, e.g. more respectful, vulnerable, kind, generous and faithful – even in times of hardship.
- What the line might be between enjoying each other's company and over-dependence in a relationship.
- What it means to be an ethical person in a relationship.
- Why compromise is important to healthy relationships.
- When we enter into a mature relationship we should go into it with heads, hearts and eyes wide open.

- How love is understood in other cultures and whether definitions of love have changed throughout history.
- How love has changed over your own lifetime, or at different stages of your own relationship.

Physical intimacy

Chat about:

- Whether they think waiting before kissing or displaying any form of physical affection is important.
- How long they believe is reasonable before touching a new partner, and how they came to that conclusion. And how they will know if their partner agrees with this.
- What they believe the role of sex is in an intimate relationship.
- Establishing consent in a romantic relationship. How they will know whether a partner has fully consented – even to a kiss – and whether they could be misreading a partner's body language.

Difficult times

Chat about:

- The unrealistic portrayal of romance in the media.
- Why people fall in love and why some people don't return their feelings.
- What it feels like not to have love returned, and how they might respond in healthy ways.
- Young people becoming too serious, too soon. Ask what they think is 'too soon' and how they decided on this age/stage.
- Friends who have abandoned their friendships and hobbies when a relationship has become all consuming. Chat about the problem with this.
- Why we can sometimes become more attracted to a person the less interested they become in us.

- Why a person can be attracted to someone who is unhealthy for them.
- Why some young people purposely choose a partner their family disapproves of.
- The pain of being cheated on and why this is so hurtful.
- What someone might do if a relationship becomes emotionally or physically abusive.

'How young is too young for a romantic relationship?'

This is something I get asked regularly, and I believe that adults shouldn't rush young teens into intense romantic relationships by trying to label their friendships along these lines. Neurologically they are still trying to figure out who they are, so it's important to encourage teens to realise that they don't need to 'find themselves' in another person.

Young teens can become clingy and over-attached when they try to find their identity or meaning in a romantic partner. I've seen many teens give up sport, activities and close friendships when a relationship becomes too intense too early. An early teen relationship in which the young couple spend all their time together, isolated from other friends and activities, is an unhealthy one, and often springs from a sense of low self-worth.

There is evidence to suggest that younger teens often experience more costs and fewer benefits when involved in a romantic relationship. Teens describe their early relationships as more stressful and less supportive, but as they get older describe their later romantic relationships as more rewarding, in terms of levels of affection, companionship and intimacy.[2] So we're not being mean when we encourage our very young teens to wait a while before getting into a romantic relationship.

Parents can help by building up their children with a sense of personal value, and encouraging them to be involved in many areas of life. Help them to maintain their friendships, hobbies, sports and other interests. Romance is only *one* dimension of us as whole people.

In the early teen years, group dates with a bunch of girls and guys in public places or homes, supervised by an adult, are a healthy and safe way for teens to get to know what kind of person they might like to have a relationship with. In these relaxed settings they learn about what they find attractive and become comfortable being themselves.

Romantic interests are normal

In saying all of the above, most young teens will certainly develop feelings for a particular person – or even a few people in one school term. It is naive of parents to think that their young teen won't have love interests at various times in their high school years. For most teens, these feelings change quickly and often. It is a normal part of growing up. What they do with that interest and how you handle your teen's emerging feelings is what matters.

It is crucial not to shut down the potential for conversations with your teen by either embarrassing them or laughing off their romantic feelings as silly or childish. Belittling your teen for having feelings is the quickest way to ensure they never come to you to talk about relationships as they get older. This is the time to acknowledge their emotions and talk about what qualities they find attractive and what qualities they don't. Chat about your time growing up and the feelings and difficulties you had, so that it does not become a time of interrogation, rather a time of sharing and age-appropriate openness.

Be respectful

It is frustrating to teens when adults label two 13-year-olds 'boyfriend and girlfriend'. Nothing kills a great friendship quicker, so please stop! Continually asking and teasing teens about a boyfriend/girlfriend when they simply enjoy hanging out with a person puts pressure on them (and they get enough pressure from their peers already). The implication is that having a romantic relationship is what defines them and they're somehow missing out or defective without one. Teens need to get the message that they're not defined by having a partner.

And please, for goodness' sake – don't go on about 'boyfriends and girlfriends' in kindergarten. Don't mess up kids' thinking by making friendships into some adult notion of romantic relationships. This teaches children that boys and girls can only be romantically involved, and can't be good friends. In the early years, encourage friendships with the opposite sex. Chat about how girls also love playing in the sandpit and boys also love doing dress-ups, and that playing together is fun. These early relationships help kids become comfortable with and develop confidence in and respect for the opposite sex.

When your child 'comes out' to you

Let me start by saying that regardless of your views on LGBTQ relationships, based on personal, cultural, or religious grounds, they are irrelevant at the precise moment your child 'comes out' to you. It's about them, not you. Your first response needs to be about listening – with unconditional love – because they are still your child. It is most unhelpful (even damaging) to launch into your own views at this point. Your child is likely to know your beliefs already. What you need to know and acknowledge is that it has taken great courage for your child to come and tell their parents something so personal – especially something they wonder about their parents' potential disagreement with. First and foremost, they need to hear that their parents love and accept them.

Why do I say that unconditional love is most important here? Because research indicates that 'LGBTQ young people are twice as likely to be diagnosed with a mental health condition, six times more likely to have suicidal thoughts and five times more likely to make an attempt on their life than their heterosexual peers.'[3] This community is struggling a great deal already. Further rejection by their parents will exacerbate their mental health struggles and will alienate them from those they need the most.

As parents, we can never assume from our stories, or others', that we know exactly what our child is feeling or thinking. A good idea is to ask open questions which show your child that you are a safe person to talk to. They need to know – really know – that you are comfortable discussing this with them, but try not to overdo it or to smother them in the process. You might have suspected this conversation would happen at some point or it might have caught you by surprise; either way, start by simply inviting your child to tell you his or her story so far.

You might begin by saying things like:

- 'I hope you know that I want you to be able to tell me anything.'
- 'I don't want you to feel I am prying – so we can have these conversations in short periods over time, if that works best for you.'
- 'Just let me know how much you want to tell me.'
- 'When did you realise this about yourself?'
- 'What are you feeling right now?'

You might also offer to help them find a counsellor, not as an indication of your rejection of them, but because a professional can offer a different level of support and guidance.

Set boundaries that make sense

When it comes to setting rules around the time your teenager spends with a new boyfriend or girlfriend, use logic and reason and respect their intelligence. Don't simply forbid certain activities or insist on times to be home – explain why you are doing so. This will help your teenager understand that you're not merely imposing arbitrary rules. Some teens may not like your most well-intentioned boundaries, but that is a normal teen reaction. Teenagers still need their parents. There's a fine balancing act between letting your teen develop autonomy and being too controlling.

First relationships are times when parents need to have those conversations about sexual curiosity, consent and being comfortable with saying no. Hopefully, this won't be the first time you're having such a conversation with your child, but if it is, don't make a big deal of it. (Read Conversation #10 for more information.) Sexual curiosity can quickly become all consuming in the intense early stage of a new relationship. Teens need to hear that sexual activity too early often breaks hearts and leaves emotional scars.

Helping teens through break-ups

Most of us remember the first time our heart was broken. It was tough. If we didn't have support it made the heartbreak even harder to bear. Rather than brushing off young break-ups as simply inevitable, we could help ease the pain, enhance our children's sense of worth and strengthen our relationships with them in the process.

It would be helpful to remind your child that:

- **Healing takes time**
Because relationships take time and emotional investment, let your teen know that getting over a heartbreak takes time too. There will often be a period of grief. Give your child permission to grieve this loss.

- **It's okay to show your emotions**
Let your child know that it is okay to cry or to express that they are in pain. Advise them to choose a few trusted people

to do this with, and not to express all of their negative feelings on social media for everyone to see, as this usually leads to further complications. If your child is displaying their pain through anger, help them to channel their emotions through positive pursuits, e.g. helping others or playing sport.

- **Connecting helps**
Let your teen know that you will give them space to be alone and process their feelings, but that too much time alone can drive them further into loneliness, so talking helps too. If not to you, then with another trusted adult. Let them know that talking often helps people process their feelings and helps them heal faster.

- **It's important to maintain your routine**
Routines bring familiarity and comfort. Keeping up with everyday chores and physical activities, as soon as possible, keeps young people from spending too much time brooding. Positive activities are helpful for a young person to realise meaning and joy again, without trying to deny they have experienced pain. Getting outside and being active can help young people feel refreshed.

Communicate to your child that it's important to:

- **Give your ex some space**
While the goal of being friends again is worthy, and even possible, this only comes with time. Make your child aware that if they were the person initiating the break-up, spending time too soon afterwards, even as friends, with an ex may give the other person false hope. If your child is the one who was let down, then space away from an ex is also important to process and get over the relationship.

- **Go slow**

Advise your child that jumping into a new relationship too soon will only lead to more pain, for your child or for the next person, who is often the 'rebound'. Remind your child that they are not defined by being in a relationship.

When your child initiates the break-up

Even if your child is the person to initiate the break-up, they may still struggle to find a new rhythm. Both parties are often left feeling a little empty and lost afterwards. If you have taught your child to have empathy, they will be keenly aware of the hurt they might cause by ending a relationship. Acknowledge to teens that breaking up will be difficult, but that it is imperative they do so in person. Ghosting (simply disappearing) or breaking up via text is absolutely not on! It will cause the other person even more pain. The other party ought to be respected enough to be told face to face, but in a clear, kind manner, without offering false hope.

If your teen becomes depressed

For some teens the emotional impact of a break-up can be overwhelming, especially if they have not developed the skills for dealing with intense emotions. If their romantic relationship was perceived to be the core relationship in their lives, which led to a distancing from friends, family or activities, this can increase a teen's vulnerability to mental health struggles.[4] For some teens this can surface a few months after the break-up, once the realisation that it is truly over sinks in.

I must emphasise, however, there is no evidence that simply being in a romantic relationship will *cause* your teen to become clinically depressed. The majority of teens will not experience a full-blown depressive episode, but if your teen becomes depressed following a break-up there will be a complex combination of risk factors to consider, and they may need a period of professional support.

- **It will get better**
Without minimising their pain, it is important that young people hear that it *will* get better. They will feel happy again.

It can be helpful to talk about break-ups in general, so that teens can better support their friends, or can be more emotionally prepared for times when they will go through one themselves.

Things you could discuss:
- Why some relationships don't work and why some people break up.
- How break-ups can be really hard, especially if you are the person not ready for the relationship to end.
- Who your teen might turn to, or what healthy activities they could engage in, as they walk through the pain of a heartbreak.
- How to break up respectfully and with care – without lashing out – despite your pain.

What if my child has made a bad choice?

One of the toughest times for a parent is when their teen has a boyfriend or girlfriend who is 'bad news' – unsuitable or engaging in dangerous behaviour. While it's tricky territory to navigate, a parent has to tread a fine line between intervening and giving their child freedom to choose and to learn from their mistakes. The level of a parent's intervention depends largely on a child's age and maturity. If your teen is still young, you have more say in when and where they see this person, as you are usually doing the driving and will have more direct supervision if they are in your home.

If you suspect (or know) there is dangerous behaviour, like drugs and underage alcohol use, among your child's peer group, don't hesitate to engage your child in a serious and direct talk. In this conversation you should be open about your concerns about where they are hanging out and with whom. You might use this time to remind them about the values your family holds and then listen to their point of view. Remind them that they can call on you at any time of the day or night if they feel as though a situation has deteriorated to dangerous levels.

For some teens there will be a period of time when you cannot change their risk-taking behaviour no matter what you say or do, and this can be heartbreaking for parents to watch. This is a time when you will need to draw on your own friends or seek professional help for support, and for more specific advice on natural consequences.

However, if your older teen or young adult child is engaging in risky behaviour with a romantic partner, it's still okay to be clear about your concerns. Yet if you are too oppressive and restrictive, and always nagging rather than listening, you will be guaranteeing secrecy, rebellion and distance. Your child will dig their heels in to try to illustrate their autonomy and prove you wrong. What you want in this situation is to have your child know that your love for them is always present and that their home is a safe place. That even though you may not agree with the behaviour of the person they have chosen, because of your family values you will be there for your child to come and talk to at any time of the day or night – without an 'I told you so!'

My biggest piece of advice to parents is: 'Don't lose your relationship with your child over something they do while young.' Be clear about your boundaries, but give up the lectures and listen more at this time. Always keep the door open for discussions and your teen will be more likely to come to you (or at least be aware they can) with questions or problems at a later stage. The aim is for a healthy parent–child relationship to continue, long into adulthood.

Key Messages

- Kids value having someone who is unafraid to have frank, open conversations. The more conversations you have, the easier the discussions become and the less likely your child will be to get into trouble further down the track.
- Build up your child with a sense of value, and encourage them to be involved in many areas of life. Help them to maintain their friendships, hobbies, sports and other interests. Romance is only *one* dimension of us as whole people.
- Teens need to get the message that they're not defined by having a partner. Having a romantic relationship is not what defines them, so make it clear they're not somehow missing out or defective without one.
- Make sure your teens know that your love for them is always present and that their home is a safe place – because of your family values, you will be there for your child to come and talk to at any time of the day or night.

Choices: 'Every choice has a consequence.'

There is an image that I use at all my seminars which has three diverging roads and the phrase, 'You are free to choose, but you are not free from the consequences of your choice.' Children (like adults) are free to choose how to behave, how to live and how to treat others, but none of us is free to choose the consequences of our behaviours. Despite the idea of YOLO (You Only Live Once) and living in the moment, every choice has a consequence that can affect ourselves – and often others. Some choices aren't life altering; choosing chocolate ice cream and then wishing you had chosen the strawberry is a temporary discomfort. But choosing to drink before driving home from a party is a different kind of choice.

Talking about consequences is not about guilt loading, or making children feel as if they can never make mistakes. Parents should always sit with arms open wide, for children to rush in after any mistake. That is unconditional love. But unconditional love cannot erase natural consequences for choices.

Natural consequences are learned in the home

Boundaries and limits teach kids that there are rewards and consequences in life. They are designed to produce children who can respect boundaries, meet responsibilities and demonstrate age-appropriate behaviour. Organisations, sports teams and orchestras run well because of rules and boundaries. No rules on the footy field is chaos, not a game. Rules teach us that others' boundaries matter.

Consequences acknowledge mutual rights and mutual respect

A consequence is something that follows naturally from a person's action, inaction or poor choice. Society believes in consequences – think of how horrified most people are when they see media stories of parents who excuse or try to buy their children out of negative consequences. For example, the American father of a former Stanford University athlete, convicted on multiple charges of sexual assault, publicly announced that his son should not have to go to prison for '20 minutes of action'. The young man later tried to appeal his conviction by excusing his sexual assault on the unconscious young woman as 'just intending to have outercourse'. The problem is that many schools and clubs are faced with parents who believe in consequences – but for other people's children, not their own, so they make excuses for their own child's poor behaviour. I have countless stories of schools where a student has been suspended for violent behaviour or for abusing other students, only to be allowed to play Xbox at home. That's a holiday, not a consequence!

We need to love our children enough to let them fail and let them face consequences for bad choices. Naturally, we need to get to the bottom of why children are choosing to behave in a negative way. Children in pain often lash out. But not allowing consequences for mistreating others while young leads to 40-year-old men who beat their wives and still blame it on their own pain. Hurt and pain are never excuses to abuse others.

We ought to love and support our kids *through* a consequence, without rescuing them *from* the consequence. By this I mean parents need to stop making excuses and defending their child when a school gives consequences for poor behaviour or incomplete tasks. Most teachers care deeply about their students and don't go into the business of teaching to make kids' lives miserable (and goodness knows they don't go into it for the money). Parents need to stop questioning schools about the boundaries put in place for uniforms, a child's inappropriate behaviour or incomplete homework. Naturally, if something is grossly unfair parents need to step in, but this should be the exception rather than the rule. Structure creates order and self-discipline.

If children don't learn to respect rules and boundaries in their schools and clubs, how will they ever know how to respect their employers, employees, co-workers, friends or lovers? Our homes, schools and clubs provide children with a soft landing; in other words, consequences that are not abusive, dangerous or life altering teach children to exercise self-control in the small things.

Self-control is like exercising a muscle. The more you use it, the stronger it becomes. This leads to better self-control in tougher areas, like being pressured to take drugs, send a naked image, or record an inappropriate encounter on your phone and post it online. Kids can learn to better contemplate a boundary and the consequences of not adhering to it before doing something hurtful or illegal. Expecting children to respect boundaries teaches them that other people matter.

Ask yourself: 'When my child makes a poor choice, are they doing it for attention, to get power, to get even or because they feel inadequate?' It's important to try to understand why a child is behaving in a certain way, so you can take the correct action. Your child must still be allowed to experience the consequence for their choice, but you can at least then address some of the underlying issues. Also, remember that appropriate consequences take time to put into action and often do not work the first time.

TRY THIS:

- The most important question you need to ask yourself when giving your child a consequence is: 'What do I want to accomplish here?'
- Stand firm and don't try to save your child from a little discomfort in the short term.
- A natural consequence should fit the behaviour in a logical way so that the child associates the consequence with the poor choice. For example, 'You took your iPad into your room and played on it after lights out. Sleep is very important to your growth and health, so you will need to go to bed half an hour earlier tomorrow night, or you will have to hand in your iPad an hour earlier tomorrow night.' The consequence of breaking the night-time technology boundary needs to be linked with the technology and the loss of sleep.
- It can be helpful to involve children in deciding on family consequences for things like not doing chores, not putting down technology at designated times or when they've physically hurt a sibling.
- Follow through with consequences, because *they teach children to link current and future behaviour.*

Selfless choice and delayed gratification

Children need to learn to sit with temporary personal discomfort, for the sake of others. For example:

- Not buying children the latest gadgets immediately.
- Waiting turns to have a treat.
- Letting someone else be first in line.
- Choosing to share their lunch money with a child who did not bring food for the day.

- Choosing to watch their sister's netball final, because they know how much it will mean to her, rather than going shopping with a mate.
- Choosing to stick with their team, even though they have lost most of the games of the season and they hate going to matches now because sleeping in would make them happier.
- Choosing to leave the fun of a party to make sure a drunk friend gets home safely.
- Choosing not to take a video of someone in an embarrassing position and posting it to Instagram to gain likes.
- Choosing to delay sex because they are not sure that someone else is ready.

Finally, we need to highlight the ability of *every* child to make good choices and use self-control. We live in a time when we're afraid to teach children to be selfless. We think we're making them weak. Yet there is nothing stronger than knowing you could make a choice for your own benefit (even if you think you won't get caught) but deciding to do something different because it is the right thing to do; this will demonstrate care and might benefit someone else. That is strength. That is true freedom of choice.

Educator Michael Grose suggests we teach children the following three tools for contemplating their behaviours:[1]

- **Is it safe?** This question helps them to assess risk.
- **Is it fair?** This question helps them to be sociable and consider others.
- **Is it smart** (and in my long-term best interests)? This question encourages them to think ahead, which isn't a typical teenager's strong point.

Children can still be kind, yet assertive at the same time. Teaching children to listen to their inner voice helps them assess whether they are being taken advantage of. Saying no to exploitation is also a strong choice.

Key Messages

- Talking about consequences is not about making children feel guilty or as if they can never make mistakes. Parents should always sit with arms open wide, for children to rush to after any mistake.
- A consequence is something that follows naturally from a person's action, inaction or poor choice. Society believes in consequences.
- Self-control is like exercising a muscle: the more you use it, the stronger it becomes. Kids can learn to better contemplate a boundary and the consequences of not adhering to it before doing something hurtful or illegal. Expecting children to respect boundaries teaches them that other people matter.

Body Image: 'Selfies, self-objectification and self-worth.'

Ever heard, 'Argh! Why is my teen always taking selfies?' Or 'Selfies lead to a generation of narcissists!' Maybe you've said it yourself?

Be assured, taking selfies does not make your teen a narcissist. There is a lot more to developing narcissistic personality disorder than smiling into a screen. Photos are part of making memories and saying, 'Look, I was here!' I remember when I travelled overseas in my mid-20s and used one of those 'modern' cameras with a timer. I balanced it precariously on a cup atop a table (so that I didn't get a shot of my bellybutton) and then ran back to my place, with Big Ben in the background.

Young people do the same today, just with a different tool. These image-sharing apps like Instagram and Snapchat allow kids to take and send photos of everything from food to friends. Whether you're on the train or at a shopping centre, teens can be seen smiling, frowning or pouting into a screen. This sharing is a normal part of today's teens' relationships and friendships. It is my belief that because we often struggle to communicate our attitudes and feelings toward something via words alone, emojis and selfies have become an effective vehicle for people to communicate their emotion and intent, when online.

I also believe that selfies and photos on Instagram feeds are just another way for teenagers to connect and identify with their peers. When we see teens sitting, heads together, chatting or laughing and looking intently at their phone screen it's no different from when we sat pouring over teen magazines or watching movies with friends. I might be giving away my age here, but we also joked about or swooned over celebrities (Morten Harket from A-ha – sigh!), debated a new fashion style (like permed 80s hair – what were we thinking?) and bonded over a song in similar ways.

In fact, research suggests that moderate use of social media might actually benefit many teens in the areas of feeling connected to their peers, developing social skills and having access to help if needed.[1]

These platforms can also be a positive outlet for self-expression and development of self-identity for many young users. Lots of young people build YouTube channels or develop themes for their feeds, which are newer forms of creativity.

The shadow side

As with anything, however, there is a negative side to image-sharing apps that we need to help our teens navigate. We can start out by reminding teens that young people, for generations, have been eager for validation and worried about what others are thinking. In the same way, everyone feels social pressure via social media at some time or another.[2] They're not alone in their love–hate relationship with it.

One example is a survey of almost 1500 young people aged 14 to 24 by the Royal Society for Public Health in the UK which sought to find out how certain social media platforms impact health and wellbeing issues.[3] They looked at issues such as anxiety, depression, self-identity and body image. What they found was Instagram, Snapchat, Facebook and Twitter all demonstrated negative effects overall on young people's mental health, while YouTube was found to have the most positive impact.

While teens enjoy the connection that Instagram brings, it topped the list in terms of negative impact, most notably among young women. One of the researchers concluded that Instagram draws young women to 'compare themselves against unrealistic, largely curated, filtered and photoshopped versions of reality'. A female respondent said in the report, 'Instagram easily makes girls and women feel as if their bodies aren't good enough as people add filters and edit their pictures in order for them to look "perfect".' The survey concluded that these apps negatively affect body image and sleep patterns, and also add to a sense of 'FOMO' (Fear of Missing Out).

When selfies become part of self-objectification

Self-objectification happens when people treat themselves as objects to be looked at and evaluated based upon their appearance, which can lead to appearance anxiety, body shame, lower self-esteem, negative mood and various forms of disordered eating.[4] As mentioned, one of the downsides of selfies is that teens feel the pressure to display perfectly curated photos, often modelled on photoshopped, posed and objectified celebrity feeds. Teens admit to taking hundreds of photos before choosing the perfect one to put online. Because apps like Instagram provide instant and measurable rewards in the form of comments and likes, teens then evaluate their worth based on the amount they receive on a photo. Many will delete a photo out of insecurity, when the responses are slow in coming. This is when posting selfies can become less about keeping up with the latest event or sharing your life with your friends and becomes more of an avenue of self-objectification.

Lindsay Kite, PhD and co-director of the Beauty Redefined Foundation, believes that this epidemic of self-objectification and constant fixation on appearance – whether someone is happy with it or not – has crippled generations of women who could have used that mental energy on much more meaningful pursuits.

The problem is the incredible power the ideal of female thinness has over us. It drives unbelievable rates of disordered eating, anxiety and depression; billions of dollars spent every year on weight loss aids that only work for 1 per cent of buyers; and troves of online 'thinspo' [thin-inspiration] and 'pro-ana' [pro-anorexia] images curated by millions of girls and women seeking value, happiness and desirability where our culture told them they could find it – thinness.

Although many girls start out posting selfies hoping to prove their body confidence, posting images of large, small and in-between bodies isn't really a solution to fighting body shame either. In doing this we're only fighting a symptom of the problem, not the root or the real cause. Kite goes on to say:

We have to understand where lasting, meaningful power comes from. It doesn't come from believing that your body looks acceptable. While that is a good feeling, and perhaps even one step closer to empowerment, there is much greater power to be found 'outside' the confines of woman-as-object, ready for evaluation and consumption. Women displaying their bodies and sharing them online – even if they look very different from mainstream ideals we're used to – is still playing within the rules of objectification. That's the same framework that has marginalized and oppressed women for as long as any of us can remember. It still depends on women being awarded arbitrary points for what their bodies look like, just with expanded guidelines for what counts as worthy of displaying or consuming. It's still others consuming those bodies – looking, evaluating, validating (through comments, likes, shares, retweets) or, all too often, mocking and harassing ...

While fighting for more bodies to be seen as acceptable (which is good and important), the photos of marginalized bodies to alleviate shame in others is one step, but it doesn't even come close to moving us out of the BODIES FIRST framework. That's where research shows it is crucial to the success of women really feeling good about themselves and overcoming the tendency to self-objectify (or remain preoccupied with their appearance throughout the day, whether they 'like' their looks or not). It's self-objectification that is hurting most women from the inside, stunting our progress ...

Positive body image isn't believing you are beautiful – in fact, it's more like believing you are 'more' than beautiful. That your body is much more valuable as an instrument for your use than as an ornament for others to admire. You don't learn that from displaying your body or admiring others' bodies, no matter what size they are. You learn that by living and doing and being, not from looking *or being* looked *at. Having positive body image isn't believing your body 'looks' good, it is believing your body 'is' good, regardless of how it looks ... You don't have to see your body as ideal in order to feel great about yourself, have loving relationships and contribute great things to the world. When a woman truly believes she is worthy and valuable as a person, regardless of the way her body looks, she will experience far greater empowerment than if she simply believes her appearance is valuable.*

I saw this very problem play out after one of my seminars. I had a girl of about 17 come up to me and say she wasn't interested in 'all this objectification nonsense'. Her goal in life was to become 'a trophy wife'. I first thought she was having me on, but she insisted that it would be the best way to become wealthy, wear designer outfits and live a fabulous social life, without having to work too hard. She just had to 'look good' for her man (and the media). I was desperately sad for this young woman, that no one in her life had told her that she was worth more than her body or looking good for someone else's benefit.

If we want to fight body shame and promote body positivity, we need to fight the lie that girls' bodies are the most important thing they have to offer. Girls need to learn to *see more* in themselves, in order to *be more* than young women who self-objectify and become preoccupied with their looks.

When body focus becomes unhealthy

Always being 'on' and connected through both traditional and social media means our children are surrounded by overt and covert messages about body image. They're inundated with a stream of messages with unrealistic narrow body types, in what we call 'the thin ideal' for girls or having the perfect build and six-pack for boys. Teeth are whitened, skin is tightened and brightened. There are food and dieting apps adding messages to their feeds telling users which foods are 'clean' and which foods aren't, which new shake will 'melt' unwanted belly fat, what exercise routine the Kardashians are doing to get beach-body ready – and on it goes. Confusion, anxiety and insecurity about their bodies are magnified through constant comparison and self-judgement.

According to psychologist Sarah McMahon, some teens struggle with subclinical eating issues as a result, and for young people at risk these can occur on the way to developing a clinical eating disorder. Subclinical eating issues involve unhealthy patterns with food and/or exercise. It might include (but is not limited to): distorted body image (seeing yourself as overweight when you are not); preoccupation with food (counting calories, obsessing about portion sizes or food groups, skipping meals); excessive dieting, purging or restricting food intake; compulsive exercise (athletes are also prone to subclinical eating disorders). Unfortunately, subclinical issues are typically overlooked, because they have become quite normal or easily disguised within everyday behaviours in our culture, and many parents struggle with these issues themselves.

If you suspect your child has developed an unhealthy obsession with their weight, body or exercise routine it is important that you gently talk to them about the patterns you have noticed. As a family you might need to develop new ways of talking about bodies and health (see 'Discussion ideas to enhance self-worth' on pages 128–129).

Body image and boys' health

Body insecurity is not just limited to our girls. Boys are more body conscious than we realise and body image issues for them are very real. Unfortunately, boys are far less likely to address their own body image concerns and are more likely to struggle alone, because body image issues have long been portrayed as a 'female' thing. Boys also tend to laugh off criticism or make a joke to cover up painful comments about their bodies, but they carry the hurt in secret.

When questioned, boys believe extreme exercise and dieting are issues for both genders, with adults slower to recognise this. Whenever I ask a group of teen boys what they think the main area of body focus for boys is, they yell out, 'A six-pack!' I've even heard 9-year-old boys talking about and trying to compare their six-packs. Boys tend to worry about how muscular they are and whether they are too skinny.

A UK survey[5] reported that although most boys say that looking good won't lead to happiness, many still believe there is a 'perfect' body to strive for, and 'perfect' means muscly, lean and athletic. Boys also tend to associate muscles with being masculine, with many boys believing they can achieve the 'perfect' body type if they work really hard for it. Paediatricians are raising concerns over the increase in muscle-enhancing behaviours in boys in particular.[6] These behaviours include steroid abuse, binge eating and exercise dependence.

The UK survey also found a general naiveté among boys about when they are being advertised to, particularly through non-traditional methods such as social media. Yet, other than friends, this is the source with the highest influence on how they dress and what it means to 'look good'. It also found that although boys say they are aware that media changes images, they tend to believe that the media changes the way women look more than men. They are often shocked by how much has been adjusted, when it is pointed out. Some boys acknowledge that the way the media portrays men is unrealistic and unhealthy, but also say it can be inspirational.

In this day and age, boys are expected to look their best; there is increased societal pressure placed upon them ... There has recently been more of an emerging market for items that were originally almost exclusively used by girls, for example cosmetics products, hair serums and sprays, hair straighteners and body hair shavers. There is some evidence that from as young as 4 years, the pressure is being felt by children too, as some are worried about eating too much causing them to 'get fat'.

This idea is called 'normative discontent'. Unfortunately, it is widely acknowledged and accepted that most women experience weight dissatisfaction. However normative discontent is now more pervasive for boys as well. This is considered to be due to the strong stereotypes of how people should look.[7]

Sarah McMahon, psychologist and director of
Bodymatters Australasia

When is it an eating disorder?

A clinical eating disorder is a complex issue, with no single cause identified (and beyond the scope of this chapter). It often includes genetic vulnerabilities, psychological factors and socio-cultural influences (social media and traditional advertising are one aspect of this).

Signs of a possible eating disorder, in both boys and girls, involve a cluster of the following behaviours:

- Weight fluctuations – up or down.
- Changes in mood, including becoming more anxious, angry, depressed or withdrawn – particularly around food.
- Increased preoccupation with body shape or weight, such as increased weighing or 'body checking'.
- Changes in eating patterns, such as eliminating food groups or specific meals; eating becoming more regimented or ritualistic; or regressive eating behaviour.
- Increased distress around meal times or eating.

Sarah McMahon, Bodymatters Australasia

If you suspect your child is at risk of developing an eating disorder, please go and talk with your GP and request a referral to a psychologist who specialises in this area.

How can we counter self-objectification and poor body image?

Encourage everyday activism

Stay in touch with what's going on in your child's world. Encourage teens to balance their social media feed by following positive role models, YouTubers and activist movements. Get involved in activist movements yourself, such as Collective Shout, eChildhood, Beauty Redefined, #thisgirlcan and International

Justice Mission. Use family dinner times to talk about the work they do and explain to your kids why they are important in shaping the world we live in.

Model body acceptance

Apart from social media and traditional advertising messages, it might be time for parents to ask ourselves: How do I regard my own body? What does my child hear me say about my body? How do we talk about food and exercise in our home?

As parents, we model self-objectification when we constantly obsess about appearances, thinness, clothing, make-up and outer appearance in general. Children quickly learn that only certain types of bodies are acceptable, and that appearance is what is most valued by their families. When we complain about wrinkles and sagging skin, we send the message that getting older is something negative and to be avoided. Little ears are listening and young eyes are watching our every move, as they attempt to make sense of and interpret their world.

Whenever I run seminars for teens I tell them this: 'In my own home, no one is allowed to say the "F" word.' They look at me and nod hesitantly, as if to say, 'Well, duh – we don't say that (out loud at least) in my home either.' Then I say, 'No – not *that* "F" word! I mean, we don't say "FAT" in my home.' We don't say things like, 'Do I look fat in this?' or 'I feel so fat!' – because fat is not a feeling. I tell teens (including my own) how sick and tired I am of the summer ads which exploit our insecurities with predictable slogans like, 'Get beach-body ready!' Ugh! Then I ask teens this: 'What exactly is beach-body ready anyway? I have a body – there's a beach. I take my body to the beach – boom – beach-body ready!'

Every body is valuable and important and worthy.

Parents and adults, please model this and unlearn the destructive messages you were taught, and learn to love your own body in the process.

How to talk to your child about their body

Parents sometimes ask me, 'What do I say if my child gains or loses weight?' Rule Number One: Don't talk to your child about their body. If your child has gained weight, say nothing. If your child has lost weight, say nothing. If a friend or family member's weight has changed, say nothing. Rather, tell your child how healthy they look. Or tell them that they are glowing. Better yet, throw out the bathroom scales and encourage children to exercise for fun and because it sends oxygen to the brain, it's good for their health, promotes better sleep and improves mood – not as a punishment and definitely not for thinness or six-packs!

Make sure you have lots of fresh fruits and vegetables in the home, because these nourish their growing bodies, but also avoid banning certain foods. Refer to some foods as celebration food or 'sometimes food', rather than 'bad' food. Help your child to learn to eat intuitively (i.e. eat when hungry and stop when you are full). Ensure your children don't skip breakfast, because not even a vehicle can run without fuel in the tank. They need food in their bodies for energy but also for their brains, so that they can concentrate at school. Poorly nourished kids and adults end up 'hangry' (angry because they're hungry). So healthy nourishment is good for their relationships too.

I recommend Dr Rick Kausman's book *If Not Dieting, Then What?* for parents who want to help their child develop a healthier relationship with food.

What about clothing and fashion?

Shopping for and wearing clothing is not inherently self-objectifying. Following the latest fashion styles is completely acceptable, if that's what you enjoy. Teens have always chosen certain styles of clothing because they want to fit in, identify with a group, display individuality or try on different identities.

Some teens will dress completely opposite from what their parents might expect for a time, while they try to develop a sense of autonomy and separate themselves from their parents. This is completely normal behaviour.

When I talk about fashion in my seminars with teens, I point out that I didn't arrive wearing a hessian sack. We talk about choosing clothes that we feel comfortable in and can move around in easily, without suddenly becoming body aware. We also talk about clothing for certain settings. For example, neither my husband nor I would wear our good leather shoes or tailored suit to the beach (unless it was a wedding, perhaps?). Equally, my university students wouldn't wear speedos or bikinis to lectures. These outfits don't match the setting.

However, we need to be especially careful about how we talk about clothing choices with girls. We must *never* imply that a girl brought on abuse because of her clothing choice.

I enjoy lovely clothes and shoes. I wear make-up and paint my nails occasionally. But being a mother to a daughter has challenged the way I engage with fashion. I grew up in a culture where women put on lipstick to check the letterbox and I didn't want my daughter growing up to focus on her appearance. I began to consciously and regularly go to the shop without make-up, or with my hair pulled into a ponytail rather than styled and blow-dried like I might have 20 years ago. I have tried to model to my daughter that we shop and choose clothing because it's fun, to express our personalities or to be creative. I am artistic – I like to paint and decorate my home – so my clothing is also an extension of that.

However, chatting in general about the concept of self-objectification, and why we choose certain types of clothing or pose for selfies, is an important part of empowering teens to see themselves as more than bodies.

Can I tell my children they are beautiful?

After a talk I gave on media messages, one mother asked me if it was okay to tell her children she thought they were beautiful, because she said when she was growing up her parents never mentioned her appearance – ever! So she grew up believing they must think she is ugly. There are so many messages telling our children that they don't measure up to narrow standards of beauty, so yes, I do believe there are times we must tell our children (both boys and girls) how beautiful they are to us. Because to me, my children are breathtaking! We should be careful not to make their appearance our main focus. We should tell them how beautiful we think their hearts and minds are – because their appearance isn't what matters most to us.

Help your child identify their Spark

The term *Spark* was coined by researcher Peter Benson.[8] Spark is what puts light in your child's eyes, fire in their bellies or gets them up in the morning. It could be anything from spending time in nature, caring for animals, the creative arts, sports, to maths and science. Ask about and seek out your child's Spark and help them to actively pursue it. Most children are able to tell you what their Spark is. Many adults have sadly forgotten or neglected theirs.

The way we help our children explore Spark is to encourage lots of interests in areas they enjoy. You and they will soon see what lights their fire. Spark also creates a focus on what a body and brain can do, rather than how a body looks. Help your children to find role models and online sites that build Spark. Also, rekindle your own Spark and talk to your children about what brings *you* life.

When your child knows what their Spark is, they become an expert in their special area, which develops confidence. It gives them something that brings them joy when peer pressure or self-doubt hit in other areas of their lives.

Discussion ideas to enhance self-worth:
- Help children develop confidence and find their voice by asking for their opinion through open-ended questions on age-appropriate topics in the media or about something that happened at school (without directly correcting their facts each time). You might even ask them for their thoughts on a small issue you are struggling with at work. Be patient and kind, because finding your voice takes practice.
- Ask, 'What's your favourite thing to do?' or 'What makes you feel alive?' – This will help your child talk about their Spark.
- Find activities that focus on what the body can do, rather than how it looks.
- Encourage exercise to *feel* good, not *look* good – treat exercise as an enjoyable part of life, not a punishment.
- Adults (including dads) – model body acceptance. Never make negative comments about your own body.
- Compliment skill and effort, not accomplishment (occasionally send your teen a complimentary text).
- Compliment your child's mind when they come up with a good idea, do well at a project, or think of something creative.
- Mention positive character traits you admire in your child – often. Ask, 'What are character or personality traits you like about yourself?'
- Teach your children to get into a habit of saying 'thank you' when someone pays them a compliment (remember to model this too – it's insulting to a person not to accept their vulnerability in complimenting you).
- Tell your children you think they are beautiful – because everything else tells them they are not beautiful enough – but mostly tell them they are *more than* beautiful.

- It's okay, even important, to tell your teens they look good in an outfit they have picked out, but *these instances should be* outweighed by the times you talk about their beautiful heart.
- Ask what they like to communicate through their dress style – creativity, individuality, fun?
- Chat about the role of selfies in sparking or alleviating self-objectification and self-consciousness.
- Talk to your daughters and sons about how advertisers, celebrities and even friends alter their images on social media to fit a narrow stereotype.
- Ask if they feel like they need a short break from social media at certain times (help them fill that time with something fun and engaging – preferably outdoors).
- Chat about their social media feed or movies you watch together and ask, 'How does that image make you feel about your body?' Talk about how images make *you* feel as an adult too.
- Model healthy technology habits by openly checking and adjusting how much time you spend on your own devices.
- Emphasise that everyone is responsible for their own thoughts and actions, no matter what someone else is wearing.
- Talk about every person having worth, even the seemingly unlovable and those we might marginalise.
- Finally, perhaps it is time to put those bathroom scales in the garage, with the other tools, only to be used for weighing luggage?

Key Messages

- Selfie sharing is a normal part of today's teens' relationships and friendships. They are a positive outlet

for self-expression and self-identity for many young users.
Teach teens that their friends also struggle with social
media messages at times too.

- Children quickly learn that only certain types of bodies
  are acceptable, and that appearance is valued by their
  families. Little ears are listening and young eyes are
  watching parents' every move, as they attempt to make
  sense of and interpret their world.

- Chatting in general about the concept of self-
  objectification, and why we choose certain types of
  clothing or pose for selfies, is an important part of
  empowering teens to see themselves as more than bodies.

- Ask about and seek out your child's Spark and help them
  to actively pursue it. When your child knows their Spark,
  it gives them something that brings them joy when peer
  pressure or self-doubt hit in other areas of their lives.

Unconditional Love: 'I will love you, no matter what!'

The greatest thing that we can do is to help someone know that they're loved and capable of loving.

– Fred Rogers

Home is the first place that children learn what love looks like. When our children are wrapped in unconditional love, the concept of worth is soaked deep into their souls. Our love needs to communicate, 'You are enough just as you are.' When our children learn that they have value, no matter what they do, whether they fail or succeed, they become more resilient in the face of adversity. Boys and girls who understand their worth grow into young adults who won't settle for friends or partners who treat them poorly.

There are many ways that we can demonstrate unconditional love to our children, and it is often within the fun and safety of family times that values are communicated and meaningful topics are explored.

Love through play

Play is the easiest way to connect to the heart of your child. Of course, play looks different in the teen years compared to the toddler years. Instead of playing cars or dress-ups, it might look like: riding a bike, video gaming, or building the chicken coop that they want – together. The key is to get into your child's world.

The 'love bomb'

'Love bomb' days or outings are dedicated, planned, one-on-one times. These might happen once a term or a few times a year and include a range of fun activities like beach crawls (one of our favourites), picnics, movies, bush walks, milkshakes or hot chocolates – all without a parent's phone present. What children love about this is that we are giving them our very precious time. It says, 'I see you', 'You have value' and 'You are valuable to me' – because every single person has a deep desire to know they have worth.

One father of six I know has dad-and-child days during the December school holidays. Each child gets to pick the places they want to visit for the day (one of the places can include an entrance fee), and what restaurant they would like to eat lunch or dinner at. They have Dad all to themselves for the entire day, and it's okay, even good, for their siblings to know their turn will come, because they are each loved uniquely and individually.

Love through traditions

Many family and cultural traditions communicate to young people that they belong to something bigger than themselves. Even when teens roll their eyes at family traditions, most feel secure in knowing that their family has special times together. These don't need to be set in stone and might evolve as your family grows and changes, but traditions communicate that we matter. There's no single tradition that brings some sort of magic, it's about making it work for your family structure. For example, you might have a very big extended family, so some traditions include the cousins, the grandparents and even a quirky uncle.

If you are new to an area or a country, some of your family traditions will only involve your little family unit, but at other times think about extending to include others who might be new or lonely themselves. I remember our first few Christmases in Australia, when we didn't have any family living in the country. We invited as many couples as we could find with small children who didn't have extended family of their own to a big Christmas Eve dinner at our home. Although my family lives near us now, we still invite people without extended family to join us all at our Christmas dinner table every year. A friend's family has a much treasured birthday tradition that includes bunting and balloons hung the night before, and the birthday person chooses whatever breakfast they would like. The family wake the person up with singing and lit birthday candles, and they all sit down to breakfast for present opening.

In his *Parenting Plan*,[1] educator Andrew Lines suggests that parents use birthdays as times to both honour their child and celebrate new milestones of growth in responsibility. I get quite sad when I hear of families that don't make a big thing of birthdays. A birthday signifies a celebration of your child's life and says you are glad they are in yours. Some ideas for birthday celebrations might include buying intentional gifts – something worthwhile and memorable which reflects your child's next stage of responsibility. You might perhaps offer a new freedom, to help your children understand the link between freedom and responsibility. This may simply be going to bed a little bit later than the previous year or being able to go a little further on their bicycle.

No matter your traditions or when they happen, children and adults enjoy the security of knowing that, even through tumultuous times, traditions serve as family anchors and safe havens to be counted on. Some family tradition ideas might include:

- Annual autumn picnics
- Monthly afternoon teas in the sun
- Annual holidays at the same beach
- Christmas Eve dinners with extended family and grandparents
- Christmas in July
- Family Passover celebrations
- Special birthday rituals
- Annual family feasts
- Dad and daughter/son nights
- Mum and daughter/son camp-outs
- Regular family dinners
- Reading together at bedtime.

There are a number of picture books to help you explore the parent–child bond together. Some of my favourites are *Guess How Much I Love You* by Sam McBratney, *Harriet, You'll Drive Me Wild!* by Mem Fox, *Owl Babies* by Martin Waddell and *Adopted and Loved Forever* by Annetta E. Dellinger.

Love through dinner-table conversations

Eating meals together as a family has wonderful benefits. Not a lot is known about exactly why family meals create benefits, but it is suggested that it is due to empathy, family cohesion, family attitudes and communication skills. The time together also generates feelings of closeness and comfort, providing a unique context to connect with your child. Although meal time on its own is not a magic bullet for emotional health, evidence suggests that children who take part in family meals display less delinquency, greater academic achievement, improved psychological wellbeing and more positive family interactions, and eat more healthy foods.

Even if your family is very busy with sport and other commitments, strive to carve out some time for family meals a few times a week. This communicates that time together is important. It appears that regular meals together, at a medium-to-high frequency (3 to 7 meals per week) reflects a sense of family connection and priorities.[2] It says, 'We are important!'

In our home, we have sit-down meals together at least three times a week. This happens even if only four out of five of us are there. We have a 'no screens at the table' rule. Another habit I've created is to expect that my kids sit together for 15 minutes at the kitchen benchtop after school for their afternoon snack at least four days a week. Again, no technology is allowed and I ask each child to tell me a little about their day. It's okay if some children don't feel like talking at every meal time, I simply ask that they do their siblings the courtesy of listening to them recount the day. My youngest is the biggest extrovert of the family – after his dad – and is just bursting to talk about his daily activities. My teens, who may or may not want to share after school, sit with us and demonstrate love and kindness by listening to his chatter for 15 minutes.

I confess that family meals that include my husband only became more regular as my children got a little older. Toddlers and young children are usually ravenous by 5 p.m., so waiting for Dad to come home later just led to hangry (hungry-angry) families. We waited until they were a little older to have family dinners and made use of Saturday afternoon teas or Sunday lunches together.

TRY THIS:

Set a goal to have a family meal at least three times per week. It could be lunch at the kitchen bench, a sandwich on your lap, or afternoon tea outside, as long as there are no screens and the focus is on the people present.

Another goal might be to include both children and adults at the table, or in a big circle of chairs, when family friends are over for a meal. This was demonstrated to me by friends who always pull together their two odd tables when people are over. They ensure that adults and children sit at meals together. Children are included in the conversation, get to watch how other families interact and also gain the benefit of incidental mentoring by being part of adults' discussions. Children don't need to sit at the table for the entire social event, but are expected to stay for the duration of the meal. My children have come to love these times.

We also need to allow for some people to choose not to chat, but just to listen to conversations. The important bit is being part of the community of the meal. It's equally okay if there is bickering or irritability some days. Families aren't robots. These instances help parents to model saying sorry, how to empathise with the person who has had a bad day, or to teach respectful communication.

Everyone's meal time will have its own family flavour – your meal time will look different from my meal time. However you choose to do it, that will form your very own family memories.

Dinner-table conversation starter ideas:
- 'List one good thing and one not very good thing that happened in your day.' It is vital that adults share some of their struggles as teens, in particular, often imagine that adults don't have inner conflict.
- 'Could we think of ways that we might help Dad deal with that situation at work?' Let children help you brainstorm. Keep it age appropriate and don't scoff at their suggestions.
- 'How did [that issue] make you feel today?'
- 'What did you enjoy most about your sport/flute/event this week?'
- 'Is there someone you are worried about at the moment?'

- 'If you could pick a non-famous person to have a dinner with, who would you choose?'
- 'If you could pick someone in history to have a meal with, who would you choose?'

If you are a little stuck with how to begin this, there are some fantastic feelings and emotion cards to use with kids and teens by Inyahead Press and St Luke's Innovative Resources. These can be used to facilitate conversations that develop expression and explore emotional intelligence.

Love means setting boundaries

One of the mistakes parents make is backing off from setting limits for the sake of short-term peace. Children feel safe and loved when they know parents care enough to give them boundaries. Of course you won't always hear, 'Wow, thanks, Mum, I really love the limits you set with my phone.'

While it is important to pick your battles, it is also important to communicate with your child why some limits might be set. Pick a few areas that are non-negotiable – they are usually health or safety related. For example, not allowing a two-year-old to play on the front lawn unsupervised; not allowing a teen to use their phone while driving (this is the law); not allowing technology in rooms at night. Some boundaries may be circumstance dependent, so will be more flexible. For example, your 9-year-old's bedtime is usually 8 p.m., but this Thursday you are out late for Grandma's 70th birthday. Other boundaries may need rethinking and readjusting as our children age, or if you come to realise you might have been too rigid.

Even when you have disagreements and times that your children go against your boundaries, reassure them that it is your job to look after their wellbeing and that their home is a safe place.

Love means knowing they can call you at 2 a.m.

It is absolutely vital that we brainstorm options for dealing with difficult situations with our children and teens before they find themselves in one. They need safe options they can draw on, rather than trying to come up with a solution in the heat of the moment.

TRY THIS:

- Let them know that you are available to do a pick-up at 2 a.m. if needed – no matter what! – because their safety is your biggest concern. Discuss some scenarios with them such as after a party, if a friend has been drinking, if *they* have been drinking, if they are left stranded, or if they want to leave an event early.
- Tell them some of your stories for getting out of bad situations, or times when you wished you could have done better in a tricky situation.
- Give them safe 'outs' for when they feel they are in a tricky situation, or if they feel they are being pressured into something they don't want to do. You could have a special emoji that means, 'Come get me now!' Or give them permission to say that they are feeling sick if they want to leave an event early. (See 'escape scripts' in Conversation #7.)

Love means saying sorry

Apologise when you overreact to something they have done – because you will sometimes (I know I have). You're only human, and you love your child, and your emotions can take over unintentionally. The problem is that our overreactions can put a wall between us and our children, ensuring they no longer talk with us on an emotional level. Don't try to justify your reaction. Just tell them you were wrong in your response and you are sorry. You can talk the situation through at a later stage. Modelling saying sorry is a powerful life lesson.

Love is an action

Through each of the avenues we use to demonstrate love, the core message is that love is an action. Love is something you *do*, not just something you *say*. This is an important lesson against abuse. When a person promises, 'But I love you,' and then goes on to *do* the opposite, that is not love. Through our actions we show our children that love does not hold grudges, love is not jealous or boastful, love is not rude or demanding. Love is never, ever abusive! Rather, love is kind, love is compassionate, love is patient, love celebrates the other person, love cares about injustice, love is hopeful, and love never gives up on you. Love your children through affectionate touch (see more in Conversation #1). Through our love, children learn *how* to love and learn not to settle for less – because people have value.

Most days this feels like a mammoth task. It is – it's parenting. But parenting isn't about doing everything perfectly every day. Perfect parents would set the bar too high for children to reach anyway. It's about the overarching message our children get from us. Children won't remember the slip-ups and mess-ups – they will remember they were loved, no matter what!

Key Messages

- When our children learn that they have value, no matter what they do, whether they fail or succeed, they become more resilient in the face of adversity. Boys and girls who understand their worth grow into young adults who value themselves.

- Spend time with your kids doing things they enjoy to demonstrate your love and to show them they matter. Think about creating special traditions you can all look forward to.
- Children feel safe and loved when they know parents care enough to give them boundaries. Even when you have disagreements and times that your children go against your boundaries, reassure them that it is your job to look after their wellbeing and that their home is a safe place.
- Through our actions we show our children that love does not hold grudges, love is not jealous or boastful, love is not rude or demanding. Love is never, ever abusive! Through our love, children learn *how* to love and learn not to settle for less – because people have value.

RAISING LOVE-ABLE CHILDREN

Respect: 'We believe in mutual rights and mutual respect.'

The truth is ... everything counts. Everything. Everything we do and everything we say. Everything helps or hurts; everything adds to or takes away from someone else.

– Countee Cullen (1903–1946)

Everyone deserves respect. Even the people we don't agree with, or who annoy us. Our children need to know that within every person lies a heart and soul, with hopes and dreams. The key to this is teaching children about personal boundaries and to treat others as they'd like to be treated.

Start by respecting your child first

It's almost impossible to expect our children to respect other people's boundaries if we don't respect theirs. Yet sometimes we forget that children are also people who deserve the same level of respect as adults. Again, it's about modelling and teaching by example. I don't mean giving children major decision-making opportunities, like how to spend the family finances; I mean affording them the level of respect appropriate for their age and stage.

For example, when your son or daughter starts asking for privacy in the bathroom, allow this. Knock before entering your teen's bedroom. If your child doesn't want a farewell kiss, simply send them off warmly, rather than taking it as a personal affront. Don't guilt trip your child into affection, or they will learn that they should shut down their instincts simply to keep other people happy. If your child doesn't want to attend an event, talk about it respectfully to find out why. A 'better offer' is not a good enough reason, but there may be another worry. Ultimately, you want your child to learn to trust that inner voice, the one that tells her when something isn't quite right. (I discussed body boundaries in more detail in Conversation #1.)

Teaching children to be respectful can be done through day-to-day modelling and activities

In the home

Parents want their children to speak to and treat them with respect, but we need to ask ourselves, 'How do I treat my own mother, or my own family?' Modelling respect also means never belittling, mocking or purposely embarrassing our children. Children will just learn to do that to others. Expect children to have good, old-fashioned manners – saying please and thank you – and remember to do the same yourself. In conversation we might ask children what they think respect looks like practically, i.e. 'How can I show you that I respect you and how can you demonstrate that you respect me?'

Teach your children to look after themselves so as not to be a burden or demand things from others as their right. Teach your son to make his own sandwiches, make his bed, clean the bath … This goes for girls too, but I mention boys as traditionally we expect this from girls and excuse boys from helping out. (Conversation #14 covers the importance of chores in more detail.)

Sibling interactions are the earliest teachable moments for respecting others. Parents can begin by modelling respect for each child by refraining from comparing achievements, abilities or behaviours, and by celebrating each child's strengths. Sibling put-downs need to be stopped, and parents can help children look for ways to demonstrate love and respect for a sibling in ways that are meaningful for each child. For example, thanking a sister for laying the table, congratulating a brother for his flute award, greeting each other every morning, saying goodnight, or lending a hand. When a child is mean or disrespectful to his brother or sister, the consequence is that they must make amends and find a way to repair the relationship. Parents can also help by finding things children can do together to build their relationship – something that brings mutual enjoyment and doesn't involve competition.

In the community

Ask children how they can recognise when they are being respected by peers or other adults. Talk about what respect looks like and feels like. In turn, ask your child how they might recognise if they are being disrespectful to someone else, and how they might look for signs that they are being disrespected. If children struggle with appropriate behaviour in certain situations, model or role-play scenarios for how to talk politely and kindly with peers, parents, the elderly, or people with a disability. It is also important to teach kindness to animals.

Mutual respect is never abusive

As part of this conversation it is vital to emphasise that respecting another person's views or choices is not the same as tolerating abuse. Don't participate in a culture of silence. If you see someone being hurt, stop and intervene, if safe to do so. Kids need to know that it's okay to speak up and to let someone know that something is wrong. Watch out for common, yet disrespectful, phrases that have been normalised by popular culture (see more in Conversation #2).

There are most certainly times when we must teach our children to say no (see Conversation #1). Demonstrate to children how to speak up by giving them scripts to say to their peers when they need to get out of a situation. Some children freeze in an emotionally charged situation and can't think of what to do. Scripts for escape can be implanted in their minds beforehand and give them something to fall back on quickly. For example, 'I forgot, I have soccer training early tomorrow, I need to leave soon,' or, 'I feel like throwing up, I need to call my mum to come and get me.'

I even encourage parents to actively give their children permission to blame them for being the 'fun police', e.g. 'My dad is such a pain, he said I can't go tonight.' Saving face is an important issue for young people – brainstorm what works for them.

Respecting sons

- Call out stereotypes when you see and hear them used.
- Speak up when others are intolerant.
- Show boys how to be tough – that is, tough enough to stand up to intolerance.
- Encourage friendships with girls. Teach your sons that girls are not mysterious or weird.
- Discuss that all girls and women they come into contact with have hopes and dreams, just like they do.
- Celebrate the achievements of girls, even if/especially when they do better than he does.
- Teach him how to properly communicate affection with kind words and gestures.
- Teach your sons to believe in and stand up for the equal rights of women.
- Model and expect apologies when someone has been hurt.

- Brainstorm escape scripts.
- Mothers need to talk to sons about how their aunt, sister, female cousin, girlfriends have felt when placed in actual situations where they were treated unfairly and as objects, simply because they are female.
- Both parents (but dads in particular) need to reinforce to their teen son that his penis does not rule his brain, because every man has the human capacity for reason, empathy and choice.

Respecting daughters

- Talk about the importance of her voice being heard and respected. Give her opportunities to speak what she feels.
- Encourage your daughter to speak up when others are intolerant.
- Teach your daughter that all boys are not gross or weird, and that there are many boys who want to get to know her heart, not just her body. Look for those boys.
- Tell her that boys and men also have hopes and dreams, just like she does.
- Explain how boys can be deeply hurt by girls.
- When someone has been hurt, model and expect apologies.
- Teach her to celebrate others' achievements.
- Brainstorm escape scripts.
- Dads should model how she should be treated by men – with respect and admiration for her abilities and talents.
- Don't ever tell your daughter that a boy must like her if he hits or hurts her. That is normalisation of abuse.
- Speak out against misogyny (see more in Conversation #12).

Key Messages

- Model mutual rights and respect for your children so they know what it looks like to be treated – and to treat others – well.
- Make sure your children know that respecting others doesn't mean they should put up with being treated badly, or allow others to be treated badly. They can say no and intervene on another's behalf, if it's safe to do so. Give them scripts to safely get them out of situations that make them uncomfortable, and give them permission to blame you, as the 'fun police'.

Media Messages: 'What do you think we can learn from media?'

The main question is not so much how the new technology can help students learn. Rather, it's what will they do with what they learn? Will they use their knowledge to build ... or will they use it to destroy? Only real human beings can help them know the difference – regardless of the medium or the technology used for communication.

– Fred Rogers[1]

Children are bombarded with media messages on a daily, if not hourly, basis. The technology itself is a neutral vehicle, although the medium is a very powerful teacher. The problem is that when we hear about some of the negative effects of exposure to certain media genres, our human tendency is to believe that *other people* are affected while we are somehow immune. This has a name: the third-person effect. As always, adults need to look at our own habits first, because we are often so steeped in the numbing entertainment of a show that we fail to recognise the extent to which we are allowing toxic messages into our lounge rooms.

It is good to recognise this about ourselves and then begin to purposely work at becoming more critical consumers of our everyday media diet.

So how do we harness the good (because there is good) and counter the bad bits that come via our screens?

Let me be clear: total restriction of teens' access to media is not the answer. My recommendation is to follow guidelines called 'Digital Nutrition' by psychologist Jocelyn Brewer:

> *Digital Nutrition emphasises the importance of balance in the way we use technology but also in considering evidence of its impacts. Imagine that activities we use technology for (apps, games, social media platforms) came with nutritional labels.*[2]

Once we consider the 'nutritional value' of the media in our homes, we are better able to gain a picture of the overall themes we are allowing to trickle into our family values.

The good news is that monitoring our children's online activity has much further-reaching effects than we realise. Research tells us that when parents become aware of and involved with their children's online activities, there is a knock-on effect of lowered overall screen time and less exposure to violent media.[3] This in turn leads to improved sleep, better school performance, an increase in pro-social behaviours and a decrease in aggression among children.

I should caution that it's not as simple as trying to ban children in their teen years from watching certain shows or playing certain games. Part of our role as parents is to assist children and teens to become critical consumers of media and popular culture. We need to help them to begin making good choices about the media they consume for themselves. Of course sometimes you will still need to step in, as this is not done in one night or with one show.

Something positive you could try is to listen to popular music with your teens. Research recently discovered this to be associated with stronger interpersonal relationships within the family,[4] but particularly with teens. On top of this, when parents and teens casually create music together, through playing an instrument or singing, this has another indirect influence on the quality of their relationship. This comes from the fact that synchronisation happens when people listen to music together, and synchronisation often causes you to like another person and empathise with them more.

It doesn't need to be complicated. When you are on your next road trip, turn up the music and sing along together.

TRY THIS:

- First, take a look at the movie and gaming diet of the entire family. Perhaps there are some changes you would like to make to your own habits?
- Use young people's everyday world. Help young children to begin to think about messages in shows, behind ads for toys or signs for fast foods. Teens can begin to decipher deeper morals and messages in video games, TV shows, movies and music lyrics.
- Chat openly about images and messages you see around you. Regularly watch movies and play games *with* your children, then talk about them afterwards. Research indicates that playing video games with your children brings a closeness, but also warns that simply watching a movie or playing a game with your child, without comment, implies that you condone all content within the show. In other words, no comment on a sexualised ad during the footy means a thumbs-up from Dad.

- Talk to teens about what they think about research that indicates media consumption is related to their evaluations of their own romantic appeal and expectations about romantic relationships.
- Listen to music with your teen.
- Chat about the music they listen to and genuinely ask – don't lecture – how they think it might make them feel about themselves and about romantic relationships, and how it portrays the roles of men and women.
- Ask children and teens if anything they have seen on a screen is worrying them, or made them feel uncomfortable.
- Use news stories (which often focus on 'bad' news) to spot strengths in people, e.g. look for people doing good things amid the bad situation, look for the helpers.
- Ask whether lyrics or musicians themselves lead your teen to evaluate their own physical attractiveness and self-worth.
- Sometimes, kindly challenge teens to take a hard look at their social media feeds, to see whether the healthy messages outweigh the unhealthy ones. Do they need to make some adjustments? Be open about whether you think you should make changes to your entertainment media habits too.

If you start to see some unhealthy thought patterns, don't jump in and try to change them all at once, or overnight. Please also don't try to rattle off all of my suggestions in one week. Pick a few things that might be relevant to your child and which you value as a family. Ask open-ended questions to help children think about why they believe something, and to highlight where there might be inconsistencies in their thinking. As your children begin to talk, really listen to their perception and interpretation of the world around them. Talk about great examples, not only poor examples, of media messages. Children will shut you out if you imply that everything media related is bad.

Discussion starters:

- 'Games and shows can be so much fun and can be something we use to relax. What shows/games are your favourites for relaxing?'
- 'I loved the positive message in that movie, I feel like it reinforces ...'
- 'Is there a character in the movie you are currently watching, that you most strongly identify with? How so?'
- 'Do you want to put your songs on in the car today? Which is your favourite?'
- 'What do you think that picture is trying to make you think/feel?'
- 'Is that ad trying to change your mind about something?'
- 'How do you think some advertising might be a bit like bullying?'
- 'How might you learn to become the boss of your own mind?'
- 'Have you ever seen something on a screen that made you feel uncomfortable? Would you like to tell me about it?'
- 'What is your favourite show/song about "love"? Can you tell me about it?'
- 'How might that song/game/movie we just watched imply that violence is a good way to solve problems?'
- 'How would we try to solve that problem in a better way, as a family?' Talk about your own views and values as a family.
- 'How does that show differ from what we believe as a family about girls/about boys?'
- 'How do you think Mummy/your sister might feel if someone spoke to her like that character did?'
- 'What do you think that music video says about the role of women?'

- 'How does this movie lie about real-life relationships?
  What do you think a person in real life would feel if this
  happened to them?'
- 'Do you notice any of your friends' games/music choices
  shaping their mood/behaviours/clothing/interactions
  with others?'
- 'Which of your favourite songs speak about strengths
  you think are important/strengths you think you have?'
- 'What is your favourite video game to play with your
  mates? What do you enjoy about playing online?'

If teens don't immediately participate in discussions after
questions you ask about media, that's okay. The fact that you
have asked something can often be enough to lead a teen to
think about an issue from a different angle.

We need to also remember that many young people don't
come to the adults in their lives when they see or hear something
inappropriate online or in the media because they fear their
devices will be removed or banned. It is important to explicitly
tell your children, 'If something makes you feel uncomfortable,
you can always come and tell me, without fearing that I will ban
you from all screens.'

Key Messages

- Consider the 'nutritional value' of the media in our
  homes to gain a picture of the overall themes trickling
  into your family values. Part of our role as parents is to
  assist children and teens to become critical consumers of
  media and popular culture themselves.
- Watch films and TV shows, and play games with your
  kids and discuss the messages they get from them. Make
  sure they understand how they support or challenge your
  family values.

Objectification: 'Love people, use things.'

Love people, not things; use things, not people.
– Spencer W. Kimball (1895–1985)

In chatting with our children about their daily media diet, we can often be tempted to focus solely on the research around the negative effects of media violence on people's thoughts, feelings and behaviours. Yet, in Conversation #8, I mentioned that media messages about love may be even more toxic, perhaps because we are not taught to view them as abnormal. A lot of our popular games and shows portray a toxic version of relationships by normalising objectification.

Objectification

'Objectification' is not a newly invented word to describe pop culture. German philosopher Immanuel Kant spoke about treating people as objects in the 1700s. Kant believed that humanity is what makes us special as human beings. It makes us capable of deciding what is valuable, and of finding ways to realise and promote our value, while objectification involves the lowering of a person, a being with humanity, to the status of an object.

In her book *Braving the Wilderness*, well-known research professor and author Brené Brown talks about this concept in terms of 'dehumanisation' – how it starts with language, often followed by images:

> *Dehumanization* [sic] *has fuelled innumerable acts of violence, human rights violations, war crimes, and genocides. It makes slavery, torture, and human trafficking possible. Dehumanizing others is the process by which we become accepting of violations against human nature, the human spirit, and, for many of us, violations against the central tenets of our faith.*

She goes on to say:

> *I know it's hard to believe that we ourselves could ever get to a place where we would exclude people from equal moral treatment, from our basic moral values, but we're fighting biology here. We're hardwired to believe what we see and to attach meaning to the words we hear. We can't pretend that every citizen who participated in or was a bystander to human atrocities was a violent psychopath. That's not possible, it's not true, and it misses the point. The point is that we are all vulnerable to the slow and insidious practice of dehumanizing, therefore we are all responsible for recognizing it and stopping it.*[1]

Both men and women can be objectified or dehumanised, but women are much more likely to be objectified in both mainstream media and in porn. When objectification is normalised, it shapes the way we see others around us.

Indeed, if girls and women are seen as sexual objects exclusively, rather than as complicated beings with many interests, talents and identities, boys have difficulty relating to them on any other level, including working together for higher causes such as volunteer work or activism, or enjoying their company as friends.

I believe we are getting a little better at recognising objectification, though unfortunately much of my generation bought into the lie that outer beauty, appearance and the thin ideal are what count. The continued popularity of shows like *Love Island* and *The Biggest Loser* are cases in point. Many adults inadvertently promote objectification because of our own habits, insecurities and unresolved issues around sexuality and worth.

Sexualisation destroys childhood

Opposition to sexualisation is often confused as anti-sex. Opposition to sexualisation is not anti-sex at all, it is anti the sexual objectification of a person. Sexualisation is recognised by the American Psychological Association as set apart from healthy sexuality.[2] Sexualisation occurs when even one of the following is present: a person's value comes from their sexual appeal or behaviour, to the exclusion of other characteristics; a person is held to a standard that equates narrowly defined physical attractiveness with being sexy; a person is sexually objectified – that is, made into a thing for others' sexual use, rather than seen as a person with the capacity for independent action and decision-making; sexuality is inappropriately imposed upon a person (this happens to children particularly).

The sexualisation of childhood is everywhere, from billboards to online adverts for swimwear. Kids and teens are saturated in these images, which infiltrate their thinking and behaviour toward others and themselves. Sexualisation is known to damage childhood by introducing issues such as body surveillance, or the constant monitoring of personal appearance, lowered ability to concentrate, devaluing of relationships and disrespect of women early on. There are clear links between hyper-sexualisation and mental health issues for both boys and girls, namely low self-esteem, depression and eating disorders (see more in

Conversation #5).[3] A sexualised climate sees fewer girls take up careers in STEM subjects. Additionally, when girls are treated as objects, they become more vulnerable to abuse.

The influence of sexualised and pornified culture changes the way boys relate to girls, shuts down a boy's emotions and distorts his view of sex. Intense body focus shapes how girls regard their own worth and how they relate to boys (covered in Conversation #5). Along with this comes a new desire to quickly mature, and even though not totally mature, young teens can give the appearance of being so by adopting adult language, mannerisms and styles.

And because many girls have bought into the pornified lie that their worth is in their bodies, they begin to believe that all boys want from them is lots of sex. Not all boys do! (More on this in Conversation #10.) I have countless stories, from parents and teachers overseas and in Australia, of young men receiving unsolicited, unrequested nudes and sexual texts from girls they know. Counsellors report girls grabbing boys' phones, stuffing them into their underwear, and then daring the boys to 'Come and get it.' Or of girls who sidle up to boys at school to show them 'dick pics' they have stored on their phones, leaving boys unsure of how to respond. During my trips to Africa, counsellors told me stories of girls sending boys images of their breasts as a form of currency. Images are captioned, 'There's more where that came from, here is my account, buy me more phone data.'

This is not okay! It is not kind. Mutual objectification is not the answer to countering female objectification; neither will it deliver equality – only mutual respect will.

We need to begin by retraining ourselves to recognise objectification and sexualisation around us, and to teach our children to immediately respond to their presence. This is imperative, as these messages quickly become a young person's inner dialogue, about both their own value as a person and the value of others.

TRY THIS:

- Focus positively on your child's character, skills, abilities and learning, above physical appearance or body shape.
- Stop self-criticism when you look in the mirror. For example, refrain from negatively referring to wrinkles, abs, bum size and breast shape.
- Make it a rule not to criticise other people's bodies, whether on the sports field or in the media. (In my opinion, *The Biggest Loser* is one of the worst culprits of this.)
- Encourage children to compliment the girls and boys in their lives for their character traits, values, skills or actions. Practise with children how to recognise these in their friends and to get into the habit of speaking positively about others.
- Employ zero tolerance of objectified language.
- Explain the term 'objectification' and that objectification happens through the viewer or consumer.
- Create opportunities for open discussions about the pressures of living in a sexualised environment.
- Find opportunities to illustrate how popular media and some fashion advertising portrays women as 'objects'. Using some of Dr Caroline Heldman's criteria, ask, 'Is the person in this image treated ...'[4]
  - like a tool or an instrument?
  - as someone lacking in freedom/autonomy?
  - as if they are interchangeable with other objects (a table, a clothes horse)?
  - without value and integrity?
  - as if they are only a body part, or only their appearance matters?
  - as if they don't have feelings or skills or dreams?
  - as something to be bought or sold?
  - essentially, as simply something to be looked at, for other people's pleasure?

- Ask your child's school what they are doing to address media literacy around sexualised culture.
- Encourage lots of other interests that focus on what a body does rather than how it looks, through sports, arts and nature.

Key Messages

- Mutual objectification is not the answer to female objectification and sexualisation; neither will it deliver equality – only mutual respect will.
- Recognise objectification and sexualisation around you and teach your children to immediately respond to their presence.

Sex Education: 'It's time we talked about sex and consent.'

> It's a travesty that political and morality wars about sex have obscured the very hopeful fact that young people want and need many uncontroversial, vital forms of romantic relationship education. Both liberal and conservative parents are on the side of healthy romantic relationships.
>
> – The Talk, *Harvard*, 2017[1]

Regardless of their views on sex, most parents I talk to wish for their child to grow up to have healthy, fulfilling romantic relationships. All parents hope that their child will grow up without vulnerability to abuse, but also that they do not inadvertently hurt someone else. So in this regard we all want the same thing for our children's relationships.

Where do we start?

We need to be cautious that in talking about sex we are not clamping down on children's healthy sexual development. Children and teens are curious about their bodies, their development and sex. Neither sex nor sexual attraction are inherently bad. They are part of normal, healthy human development. We ought to be encouraging young people to be safe, healthy and confident about their bodies and sexual development. The problem is that the sexualised wallpaper of society does not allow for this natural development to occur in our kids. With the internet reported by many young people as their most trusted source of information on sex education[2] and many tuning in to pornography, young teens are forced into an early awareness of unhealthy sexual practices.[3] Young people have questions; they may talk to peers, but their peers are turning to the same broken sources as they are. Young people need strong alternative voices to those of Pornland. Parents should arm young people with lots of information about sex and relationships. More information does not lead to sex-crazed teens going out to 'try it out'. In fact, when teens have information about sex they are more aware of the complexities of engaging in a sexual relationship and are likely to delay sexual encounters.[4] They are also more empowered to say no when they are not ready or when they feel coerced.

How adults are failing young people with sex education

Yes, children's decisions might be fuelled by porn culture, but I also believe that adults are failing youth in a big way. We either tell them nothing at all or we push them into sexual experiences way too soon. We give them mixed messages about sex and relationships all the time. For example, a small but loud minority imply that lots of opportunities for exploring sexual individualism leads to empowerment. They say, 'Sex is just a physical thing and we need to actively encourage teen sexual exploration. So go on teens, do what feels right for *you*.'

This is a problem because as we continue to peddle selfish sex masquerading as freedom of expression, based largely upon seeking *my* pleasures, *my* desires and *my* appetites, we sell our young people short. Teens are told, 'Have sex when *you* are ready!' but we forget to teach them to question how to be certain that the person they are with is also ready. How do they know they are not imposing their desires (or images) on someone else? How do they know that good sex requires intimate communication or needs a certain level of commitment to be able to do so? When we admonish youth to ignore that old adage about future consequences and tell them that future sexual regrets are simply the product of imposed guilt, enforced by the fun police (I am one of those, apparently) who have forgotten what it was like to be young, we set them up for heartache.

Yes, young people should absolutely hear that 'sex is about pleasure'. But when they learn (through porn, other media and even some adults) that sex is about 'me' and 'my pleasure', lacking connection or relationship, we are only guaranteed two possible scenarios:

1. They will have been used

or

2. They will use someone else.

I witnessed this issue of early sexual encouragement recently, when a parent's complaint about a harm minimisation approach, in a school's 'Respectful Relationships' program, was published in the national news.[5] The school taught that delaying sex was an option, to their year 8 students (their school reportedly only went to Year 9 at the time). The parent believed that teaching a child to delay sexual activity was 'archaic'. To be clear, the school didn't say 'don't ever have sex' or 'sex is bad', they suggested 'delay'. It is important to keep in mind that the teens they spoke to would have been between 13 and 14 years old at the time of the report. Although many children's bodies are hitting puberty around 13 (some as early as 10), a number of

13-year-old girls wouldn't have had their first period yet. I teach sexuality education classes and still have 12-year-olds giggling or hiding their faces when I show pictures of penises and vulvas. I have even had the occasional student faint when we talk about periods. Most 13-year-olds haven't even had a girlfriend or boyfriend, or held someone's hand, and they're still trying to figure out how to have a proper conversation with their crush. Sexual maturity doesn't suddenly drop into their laps with their first 'wet dream'. When the research indicates that most young people regret their first sexual experience because it was rushed, painful or forced,[6] why wouldn't adults discuss a delay as an option?

How poor-quality sex education hurts girls

For too long women were put in danger because they were taught to simply do what their men asked of them. They were told that 'good girls' don't think about (or even like) sex. This was in no way healthy, but I'm not sure the normalisation of porn culture has left our girls any better off. Girls still report their role in sex as largely passive, with not much agency or choice. This leaves girls vulnerable to exploitation.

Unfortunately, in response to generations of destructive male sexual dominance, we see adults design poorly thought-through school programs in the name of pseudo female empowerment. One such program taught 12-year-old girls how to engage in the 'Art of safe sexting'[7] (sexting is discussed in Conversation #11 in more detail). Can you imagine the outcry if a male educator designed a program teaching boys how to send 'safe dick pics' to girls? So we see girls uploading bedroom selfies, post-sex, sometimes with multiple boys – and celebrating this as female sexual empowerment. Perhaps in the belief that aiming objectification at boys will somehow balance the problem of men having dominated sexually for decades? When all it does is lead to teenage pain.

Behind closed doors, my colleagues and I see these hurting young teens, disillusioned and numbed by sex. Many young girls are at best bewildered and at worst regretful of their first sexual experience, oftentimes when drinking alcohol was involved. We have some girls wondering why none of the boys were tender or kind to them after sex, and others trying to figure out why they are being ignored in the school grounds by the same boy they sent naked photos to. Many say they are happy to never have sex again. When asked, 'How did *you* feel when you had sex?' these girls look at you in confusion, because it never occurred to them that sex was something that they had a say in, or could even say no to. Sex for them was something transactional, rather than relational. It was something they were required to give for affection, status, to feel loved, to fit in, to look hot, 'because they should', or to gain some empty type of 'empowerment'. All this puts them at risk.

Data shows that significantly more girls than boys are receiving anal sex, despite the fact that most girls don't enjoy it and find their first experiences to be painful, risky and coercive.[8] In other words, girls are often pushed by boys into allowing this practice, with both parties expecting it to be unpleasant for the girl. Key themes among teens about heterosexual anal sex appear to normalise coercion and 'accidental' penetration and competition among boys. The phrase 'every hole's a goal', used by teens, illustrates this point. Anecdotally, GPs put their hands up at my seminars to verify the statistics, saying they have more girls presenting with anal tears than ever before. Girls have come to believe that they simply have to accept or perform sexual acts that are humiliating or painful.

Teen girls are terrified of their partner being angry,[9] they fear being rejected or isolated, so they just say 'yes' because they think that's what modern girls are meant to do. We need to teach girls that they are more than just bodies.

How poor-quality sex education hurts boys

By 13 or 14, boys have strong sexual feelings and if no one is talking to them or deciphering what they see on the web or hear through their friends, the messages can be confusing and wrongly interpreted.

— A/Prof. Michael Nagel, PhD, author and educator

Boys are often laughed off as testosterone-fuelled animals, wanting nothing but sex. These assumptions can shape how parents approach the conversation of sex and intimacy with their sons.

Because of the way we bring up our boys, sex can become the more socially acceptable way for boys to gain some of the affection they crave, albeit poorly. Mark Greene of Remaking Manhood says:

[S]ex speaks to the wounded little boy and his endless appetite for me, me, me. And drowned out by our relentless emphasis on sex, every other gesture of caring in all the other parts of our relationships are not marked. Are not valued. Instead the only marker of a good relationship is frequency of sex. Which, because we avoid emotional intimacy, is fuelled by the cartoon daydreams of porn instead of the deeper resonance of love. Men using sex as a way to bridge their way back to the gentle comforting connection of our distant childhoods.[10]

He goes on to say that the problem with this is that sex becomes another exercise in internalising boys' experiences, instead of surrendering to the potential for interdependence. Like everything else in their emotional landscapes, boys begin to confuse the ghost of sexual contact with really connecting.

In contrast to what I mentioned about girls, it is far less likely that we will see boys in our offices to talk about issues on sex – because boys are socialised and shamed into never admitting that they didn't enjoy, or might not have wanted, sex in the first place. So they quietly implode – with mental health, body image or relational problems.

Believe it or not, boys can also feel pressured into having unwanted sex. This hurts boys just as much as it hurts girls! The journal *Psychology of Men and Masculinity*® found[11] that 45 per cent of high-school and college boys reported unwanted sexual experiences, with 95 per cent of those involving a female acquaintance as the aggressor. Thirty-one per cent of the boys in the study said they were verbally coerced, 26 per cent described unwanted seduction through sexual behaviours and 7 per cent said they were compelled after being given alcohol or drugs.

Sadly, unwanted seduction of boys is largely overlooked and underreported in the media, as it is assumed that boys always want. Now, I am not denying that teen boys do *think* about sex – a lot – but that doesn't mean they welcome all sexual advances and *want* to actually go out and have sex all the time. According to the report, boys find it difficult to talk openly about coercion because of peer pressure and their own sense of an obligation – in no small measure fuelled by the messages in porn. (I personally wonder if these numbers are actually higher, because of boys' fear of appearing weak or odd at reporting unwanted sexual contact and attention from sexually aggressive girls or guys.)

On the other hand, when boys do things that express this sexual independence that some adults encourage as 'just what boys do', they're crucified. Adults gasp at reports of teens living out this 'me, me, me', individualistic-appetite sex culture: boys from 'top' schools taking and posting online videos of their sexual conquests; young men sharing a gang rape of a drunk girl or boys creating a slut-shaming and sexual conquest–rating page. We wonder how they got to the point of making these heinous choices. (In no way does this excuse their behaviour, and such behaviour should be met with serious consequences.) However, this didn't happen by chance – it's what we get when we tell teens, 'Go and do what feels right for *you*.'

As a society, we value sexual independence, yet we know without a doubt that sex is not purely an individual, physiological component of our humanness. We realise this because of our response to the pain caused by issues such as infidelity. Any sexual experience is deeply entwined with the human psyche and the human spirit. Without teaching about communication, intimacy and trust, we risk young people encroaching on the freedoms of another person.

What can we do about it?

Sex is not a topic we are going to get universal agreement on – I am fully aware of that. But we must at least begin to teach our young people that both individuals in a relationship matter, and that sex requires intimate, two-way conversation.

Talking to teens about sex

Incredibly, most modern teens have never had conversations with their parents about the link between being an ethical person, romantic relationships and sex. Yet two-thirds of teens believe they are more comfortable talking about sex than their parents' generation.[12]

Unfortunately, we know that many kids still learn about sex from the internet before their parents work up the courage to have 'the talk'. We need to be clear and direct with our teens instead of just sneaking a how-to book onto their beds and assuming they will figure it out. It's really difficult to figure it out when you're young and getting conflicting messages from peers and media, without anyone reliable as a sounding board to wrestle with those messages.

The great news is that a Canadian study found that almost half of teenagers consider their parents to be their sexuality role model, far ahead of peers.[13] The findings obviously blew apart the long-accepted stereotype that when it comes to sex, children are mostly influenced by peers and celebrities. The study went on to show that less than one-third were influenced by their friends and only 15 per cent were inspired by celebrities. This landmark survey also revealed that most of the teenagers who looked to their parents lived in families where sexuality was openly discussed and so had a greater awareness of the risks and consequences of STIs.

Children who are well informed and comfortable talking about sexuality with their parents are also the least likely to have intercourse when they are young adolescents. This again disproves the myth that our children will go out and experiment more if they have more information about sex. Teens also describe an increased ability to 'handle pornography satisfactorily' if they had developed positive relationships with others, specifically friends and family.[14] There is a link between good communication between parents and children and more responsible choices around sexual behaviours and pornography use.

However, our parental concern about the negative consequences of sexual activity shouldn't reduce our talks to a laundry list of 'don'ts': *don't get a sexually transmitted infection; don't get pregnant; don't get a girl pregnant.* As important as these topics are, they can become the focus and we lose valuable opportunities to talk about love, kindness and care in relationships. Failing to talk about the pleasurable side of sex (as scary as that may seem) can damage parents' credibility. When we only talk about the dangers, teens will devalue everything else we have to say.

Young people learn very quickly what is okay and what is not okay to talk about, based on topics we are silent about. When they can't get anyone to talk about sex or the sexual feelings they are developing, all they are left with are the images they find on the internet.

This research tells us that almost one-third of young people surveyed had never had any of the following conversations with their parents:

- Being a caring and respectful sexual partner.
- Being sure a partner wants to have sex and is comfortable doing so before having sex.
- The importance of not pressuring someone to have sex with you.
- Assuring their own comfort before engaging in sex.
- The importance of not continuing to ask someone to have sex after they have said no.
- The importance of not having sex with someone who is too intoxicated or impaired to make a decision about sex.

So be encouraged: anything we do from here on is going to be better than what has been done so far.

The biology

To even define sex is difficult, because it is a complex aspect of human nature. Hence, whatever I say here is bound to ruffle some people – one way or the other. I will start by mentioning that there is no research which has been able to easily document universal sexual trends. Phew! – no wonder we all find it so hard to define exactly. Sexual trends and behaviours are different depending on culture, region and sex.[15] One thing we do know is that parents and families play a central role in the ways young people become sexual.[16]

The reports on teen sexual activity are mixed. Some show that teens' sexual experiences still occur at about the same age as in previous generations.[17] More recent studies[18] report a general reduction in (in-the-flesh) sexual activity from many parts of the world, including Finland, Japan and the US. The US study,[19] which analysed the responses of over 8 million teenagers between 1976 and 2016, suggests that teens have fewer sexual partners and are starting to have sex later than their parents' generation.

More specifically, the percentage of American 9th to 12th graders who said they had not had sexual intercourse increased from 46 per cent in 1991 to 60.5 per cent in 2017.[20] Data from the National Survey of Sexual Health and Behavior (NSSHB) report rates of vaginal intercourse among 14 to 15-year-olds to be a rare event, with 90 per cent of males and 88 per cent of females reporting never having engaged in such sex.[21] An Australian study[22] indicates that about 25 per cent of Year 10 students, a third of Year 11s and 50 per cent of Year 12s reported having had sex.

What's interesting to me about these studies is that a significant proportion of young people are choosing *not* to engage in sexual activity while at school, and say they are not ashamed to say so.

However, some experts point out that these reports don't show the full picture because, although Western teen pregnancy and birth rates have declined, sexually transmitted infections are up, as are reports of anal sex.[23, 24]

Fully understanding young people's sexual behaviour might be uncertain because 'sexual intercourse' is the term many researchers use when surveying young people about sex, and there is no universal definition of what counts as sex. Some teens might say it wasn't sex because it was very quick, or because nobody had an orgasm, or because it wasn't penetrative. Some might say oral sex is not sex.

So – let's just say it's complicated!

It goes without saying that STIs and pregnancy are part of the necessary discussions about sex; however, many young people in my seminars don't realise that sexually transmitted infections are transferred through both oral and anal sex. Many have never been challenged to consider that sexual coercion could involve oral and anal sex. That coercion and pressure for these behaviours is still wrong. It is also very concerning that 25 per cent of sexually active students report an experience of unwanted sex of some kind.

Even if teens are not having more sex at earlier ages, or more often than their parents' generation, the stats indicate that sexual activity still increases with each age at high school. I am also gravely concerned about the normalisation of sexualised media and porn, and how these are shaping our young people's ideas about sex and relationships, and how this will play out when they eventually do have a sexual relationship (more on pornography in Conversation 13). So it is important that we ask young people directly and speak plainly, about both the physical and relational dimensions of sex.

TRY THIS:

Both boys and girls need help to understand and embrace their own emerging feelings as they enter teen years, and not be made to feel weird or ashamed about their love interests, crushes or body changes.

- Talk to your teens about what you believe constitutes sex and ask what they believe is part of sex.
- Discuss what they know about oral and anal sex.
- Use media messages to frame conversations. Talk about how media defines 'sexy' and pushes the message that casual sex is just what you do in relationships.
- Ask how your teen decides what their boundaries are.
- Ask how they will know for certain what their future partners' boundaries are.
- Girls especially need to hear that they don't *have to* have anal sex.

- Boys need to hear that they can also refuse sexual advances.
- Make sure they know that choosing not to have sex can also be empowering.
- Give your teens ideas for ways out, to save face, when they feel pressured – 'I've just got a text from my mum/dad/brother, so I have to get home now.' Or 'I've got an early shift/game/class tomorrow.'
- Remind your teen that another person's body belongs only to them. You have no claim to it, no matter how long you've been dating. Every person makes the rules regarding their own body. In the same way, you make the rules concerning your body.

Don't always talk in the abstract. It's great to use examples from media, but sometimes kids need you to ask: 'How are you going to make decisions about what you do and don't do sexually?' Sounds terrifying, I know, but this is what college students have said they wanted and needed. You don't have to ask them to tell you where their boundaries are going to be, but ask them to make decisions about that, and to talk with their romantic partners about it. Every single time I've done that, the teenager has come back and told me that they were so glad that they'd had that conversation.

– Prof. Jennifer Shewmaker, US psychologist

The 'm' word – masturbation

At every single talk I give to high-school students I invite them to put anonymous questions into a box, which I promise to answer during a Q&A session at the end. I always reassure them that nothing they say can shock me, and that chances are I have had their question asked a number of times already over the years. At *every* seminar on sexuality, I get asked about masturbation. They usually want to know if it's okay, or if it's normal, or if they are 'bad' for doing it.

I am not going to say a whole lot about masturbation, other than that every teen will do it at some point or another, as they discover their own emerging body responses. If we make teens feel guilty or ashamed about it, especially in religious communities, they will simply do it anyway, not ask questions about it and then be weighed down with guilt. Of course anything that becomes obsessive is unhealthy, but there are far bigger things to worry about than whether a teen is discovering that their body responds in certain ways. So talk about it – at least once – but please avoid shaming your child in any way.

My biggest concern (which needs to be part of your conversation) is the link between masturbation and pornography. We need to strongly talk to teens about this danger. When their emerging sexual arousal becomes linked with porn viewing and the dehumanisation, abuse and objectification of another person, this creates a difficult and dangerous chain to break. (Pornography is discussed in Conversation #13.)

Verbal consent is not enough

Explain to teens it's not just 'no means no' because that's entirely too low a standard, particularly as alcohol is too often involved.

– Liz Walker, sexologist

We teach children that to verify consent they need to hear 'yes' and understand that 'no means no!' Except that even very young children and teens I talk with easily tell me that yes doesn't always mean yes. They know that people can say yes when they feel pressure to fit in, to be liked, to look cool, because of fear, or due to an imbalance of power. And sometimes saying no can be very difficult for some people.

So we are selling our children short by teaching them at 14 years old, 'all you need to hear is a resounding yes to understand if an individual provides consent'. This gives them a pathetic success rate of correctly interpreting consent. This false reassurance is inaccurate and unethical.

In an article for *The Washington Post*, Professor Jonathan Zimmerman asked the question about consent that so many of us had been struggling to articulate: 'We're casual about sex and serious about consent. But is it working?'[25]

But I've got a different question, one which you don't hear nearly as often: If boy and girl don't really know each other, how could they know what each other really wants?

That's a question about intimacy, not just about consent ... University administrators take it for granted that a certain amount of sex will be 'casual,' that is, devoid of intimate emotion or connection. But our rules now require the sharing of feelings, even in an encounter that is by definition divorced from them. We simply assume that virtual strangers will be having sex. But we urge them – or, even legally enjoin them – to communicate openly and explicitly about it.

Good luck with that. We might succeed in cajoling more students into some kind of verbal consent. But that's a script, a bedroom contract between sexual vendors. Yes, it will make the whole transaction legal. But consensual? Really? If you met somebody an hour ago, how can you tell what they want? And since you know so little about them, aren't you more likely to do something that they don't want, no matter what kind of 'consent' they have given?

I'd like to suggest a modest addition to our campaigns against sexual assault on campus: Instead of simply pleading

with students to ask for explicit consent when having sex,
we should be asking them why they are having sex in the
first place ... But if we want to protect our students, not just
their colleges, we will have to begin a deeper dialogue about
the meaning of sex itself. Who wants to have sex, and why?
And who really benefits from a 'friends-with-benefits' system?
When we separate physical intimacy from the emotional kind,
we provide a fertile soil for sexual miscommunication and,
yes, sexual coercion. For the past several years, we've tried to
be casual about sex but serious about consent. And it's not
working.

When alcohol is involved

Encouragingly, it has been reported that teens today are making better choices with alcohol than previous generations. A number of studies, both in Australia[26] and the US,[27] show more teens choosing not to drink, regardless of gender or socio-economic background. However, there are still some concerns in the UK[28] where although teens appear to be drinking less than in the past, they are still getting drunk more often and consuming larger quantities of alcohol than most of their European peers.[29]

Why am I talking about drinking trends in a chapter on sex? Because something we also know is that although fewer teens are choosing to drink, those who do are drinking at dangerous levels. Given the detrimental effects of alcohol on the developing brain and the numbing fog that comes with consuming alcohol, we need to continue to warn young people about its dangers. Alcohol lowers inhibitions, which can make it more likely for teenagers to make risky decisions, with half of sexual victimisation incidents involving alcohol.[30] We still see far too many acts of abuse and harassment occur during alcohol-soaked gatherings.

*Certainly I believe that this is a generation that really wants
to look after others, most particularly their friends. Girls
are more likely to ask for information on how to look after
their friends, particularly when they are drunk, but in my
experience boys are just as likely to assist in an emergency and
are more likely to do it by themselves. Girls tend to operate in
'packs' and as a result, no one necessarily takes the lead and
that's where things can go wrong.*

*Unfortunately, young men's attitudes toward alcohol are a
reflection of what we see in the general community, and even
though they truly care about themselves and their friends,
when alcohol is added to the equation, their value system can
change and their attitudes, particularly toward young women
who like to drink, can be frightening.*[31]

– Paul Dillon, founder of DARTA
(Drug and Alcohol Research and Training Australia).

What can we do?

We should start by modelling healthy choices with alcohol
ourselves and openly talk about our *feelings and thoughts on
underage drinking.*

If your child is in high school, it is a good time to start
with discussions about alcohol at parties and what they think
they might do if offered a drink. Peer pressure is a major
factor in teens' choices around alcohol, but when teens get
to hear about the negative effects of alcohol on their health
and relationships, and that their generation is making better
choices than ever with alcohol, they can (and do) make more
informed decisions.

This is where our value system (mentioned in Chapter 3)
should impact the rules and boundaries we set around alcohol.
Especially because one of the game changers for many teens

now choosing not to drink is the reduction in parent supply.[32, 33] Parents have become aware of the risks. We now understand that parents are one of the main suppliers of alcohol to young teen drinkers. It comes from the mistaken belief that providing their younger teenager with alcohol will help their child to drink 'more responsibly', because they are 'under supervision' and they will then make better drinking choices when going out. This actually has the opposite effect: these teens tend to drink higher quantities of alcohol when out.[34]

We also need to help our young people come up with safe 'outs' for when they are in situations where drinking is involved. Telling teens to 'Just say no' is very difficult for many to do in reality. You might help them come up with scripts they could say, to get out of a tricky situation. For example, they could make an excuse about having sport or work the next day and needing a clear head; feign illness, or volunteer to be the designated driver once they get their driver's licence.

I tell teens about the time I was offered alcohol at a party when I was 14. The alcohol was bought and supplied by the parent, who often wanted to be seen as 'the cool mum'. The power imbalance was enormous in having an adult encourage the young girls to drink. I spent the party walking around with the same can in my hand, pretending I had just picked up a new one. During the course of the night I slowly disposed of the contents into the indoor pot plants. Ideas and stories help teens think of creative ways to stick with their values, but also not feel embarrassed. They help teens realise they are not alone in choosing not to drink.

It is important that both parents, whether together or not, are on the same page in this area. This may take some compromising and discussion, but you need to remember your child's safety is paramount!

In conversation

- 'When someone says no, respect that no. And don't ask again.' Give your child some age-appropriate scenarios here. For example, 'No, I don't want to play that game.' Or 'No, I don't want a hug.'
- 'In what situation do you think a person might say yes when they actually want to say no?'
- 'It's never okay to touch someone, cuddle someone or take their hand if they don't want you to do it.'
- 'It's never okay to push someone else to do something they don't want to do.'
- Ask whether they believe someone can use the words, 'But I love you,' or 'Don't you love me?' in a manipulative way.
- 'Everybody deserves respect. What do you think respect might look like for [Sally, John, your teacher, Grandma, the cat]?'
- 'Boys can and do say no.'
- 'Do you know what "no" looks like in someone's body language?'
- 'A person who is drunk can *never* give consent!'
- 'Hey, did you realise that your generation is making better decisions around alcohol than my generation did? That's amazing. Have you heard about that?'
- 'What would you and your friends do at a party if you saw a guy/guys taking a drunk girl off on her own?' 'What do you think you could do?'
- 'Do you know what "no" looks like on someone's face or in their tone of voice?' Model or role-play this, as even teens struggle to figure out different facial expressions, especially those who are on the autism spectrum.

Relationships and emotional attachment

The truth is that sex is both more important and less important than our culture makes it out to be. It's more important in that, at its best, it has meaning and emotional power. And it's less important in that it is by no means the only important aspect of life or of love.

– Jean Kilbourne, Ed.D., in *Killing Us Softly*

Young people are led to believe that sex is easily divorced from emotional attachment. Yet this is probably the most important aspect of sexual relationships that we leave out of our discussions with teens. We need to teach that sexual relationships involve communication and vulnerability, and that sex involves the whole person. Steve Biddulph encourages us to teach young people about a 'happy sexuality'. If we care for our youth, we need to encourage sexual relationships that exist within boundaries: the boundaries of mutual love, mutual respect, mutual caring, mutual self-control, mutual commitment and mutual maturity. 'Happy sexuality' can't happen for just one person in a relationship, because then it's not really 'happy'. Only when sex and sexual choices become about others also, and not just our own desires and appetites, will we see a difference in objectification, rape culture and the porn industry.

TRY THIS:

- Talk about subtleties in relationships such as love, lust and like.
- Ask what commitment means to them.
- Let your teen know that it's okay to think about sex and to feel sexual desire – everyone does. It's how we are designed.

- Explain that sexual desire is not bad – it's what you do with that desire that matters – especially if it's only all about you.
- If you believe sex is important in a long-term relationship, discuss why you think this.
- Emphasise that actually liking a romantic partner is an important part of being with a person.
- Talk about people as complex beings, so sexual encounters touch the whole person, not just the physical parts of us.
- Emphasise that unless a person is asking someone for advice, talking or bragging about their sexual relationship is disrespectful and potentially damaging to a partner.
- Encourage teens to ask themselves, 'If sex is all about the individual, what does "the individual" I am with care about? What do they like? And do they care about me as an individual, too?'
- Ask your teen to consider why some people might prefer to wait before having sex.
- Emphasise that sex shouldn't be a performance. Explain that sex in the right context is beautiful, exciting, giving and pleasurable.

There are positive messages our teens need to hear about sex, lest the common myths put pressure on them that they don't want or need. It is vital that we teach young people that sex should involve love, happy sexuality, intimacy, sharing, mutual enjoyment and strong commitment.

Key Messages

- Parents should arm young people with lots of information about sex and relationships. More information does not lead to sex-crazed teens going out to 'try it out'. When teens have information about sex they are more aware of the complexities of engaging in a sexual relationship and are likely to delay sexual encounters.
- Ensure your kids know that sex should involve communication, intimacy and trust so that it is not a selfish act – just about what *they* want – but is an experience they share with another person. Sex includes an intimate, two-way conversation.
- Children who are well informed and comfortable talking about sexuality with their parents are less likely to have intercourse when they are young adolescents and have a greater awareness of the risks and consequences of STIs.
- Talk about masturbation at least once. Never shame or embarrass a teen about it. It is the link with porn and objectification that is most destructive.
- Kids need to know that saying yes or no isn't enough when discussing consent.
- Only when sex and sexual choices become about others also, and not just our own desires and appetites, will we see a difference in objectification, rape culture and the porn industry.

CONVERSATION #11

The Hook-up Myth: 'Not everyone is hooking up or having casual sex.'

Before launching into the topic of hook-ups, first ask your teen what their idea of 'hooking up' is. Most recognise it as a very broad term that covers anything from kissing at a party to oral sex to intercourse. But one thing is clear: they all recognise it as something outside the bounds of a relationship – teens don't refer to kissing a girlfriend, for example, as 'hooking up'.

The good news is despite our adult hand-wringing, there is no crazy hook-up epidemic. Really!

Certainly, there's no question that *some* young people are hooking up frequently, and some even report positive feelings after a hook-up. However, especially when combined with alcohol or drugs, hooking up can lead to serious harm. One study on college students indicates that most of their unwanted and nonconsensual sex occurred in the context of hook-ups, particularly when alcohol was involved. The greater the alcohol use, the more likely nonconsensual penetrative sexual hook-ups (rather than non-penetrative sexual hook-ups) occurred.[1] Adults must work to prevent these harms. However, the fact is that far fewer young people are hooking up than teens and adults commonly imagine; this behaviour is far from the norm.

Harvard research indicates that teens and adults greatly overestimate the size of hook-up culture and casual sex.[2] A large majority of young people are not hooking up frequently and 85 per cent of young people prefer other options to hooking up, such as spending time with friends. Most of those surveyed said they would prefer to have sex in a serious relationship. The survey also asked students about their ideal Friday night, and offered the following choices: sex within a serious relationship; sex with a friend; sex with a stranger; hooking up (but not sex); going on a date or spending time with a romantic partner; hanging out with friends; spending time alone; or something else. Only 16 per cent chose an option related to casual sex; 10 per cent wanted to have sex with a friend; 4 per cent wanted to have sex with a stranger; and only 2 per cent wanted to hook up. The remaining 84 per cent of respondents reported either wanting to have sex in a serious relationship, or chose an option that did not involve sex. Females were less likely than males to be interested in casual sex but, contrary to the stereotype, large majorities of males also did not choose one of the options related to sex or hooking up.

Michael Kimmel, author of *Guyland*, reports similar misperceptions: 'I asked guys all across the country what they think is the percentage of guys on their campus who had sex on any given weekend. The average answer I heard was about 80 per cent ... The actual percentage on any given weekend is closer to 5 to 10 per cent.'[3]

How the hook-up myth is detrimental to teens

In line with my thoughts on the pain caused by an individualistic sexual culture, the previously mentioned Harvard survey found that many young people hook up with higher expectations about intimacy and commitment than their partner, which results in them feeling betrayed and disillusioned. On interviewing girls, well-known author and researcher Peggy Ornstein found that casual sex is often narrowly focused on male pleasure. This leaves girls both confused about sex and vulnerable to abuse, and this damage can be taken into their adult relationships. However, emotional pain is not only experienced by girls. Both research and conversations with young men indicate that boys tend to be more interested in and anxious about romance than is commonly believed. Boys are keenly interested in human connection, and hook-up culture can leave them with the pressure and shame of not keeping up with the fictional idea of male sexual prowess.

The overestimation of casual sex and frequency of hook-ups leads to teens' and young adults' self-doubt, embarrassment or shame, because they wrongly believe that they are not keeping up with the so-called norms of their peers. It can also pressure teens to twist themselves into anxious human pretzels in order to engage in sex they are neither ready for nor interested in, just to fit the norms of porn-induced culture.

Essentially, the American Psychological Association concludes, 'By definition, sexual hookups [sic] provide the allure of sex without strings attached. Despite their increasing social acceptability, however, developing research suggests that sexual hookups may leave more strings attached than many participants might first assume.'[4]

TRY THIS:

- Ask teens what they hear about hook-ups in their peer group.
- Talk to teens about the hook-up myth: 'Did you know that not *everyone* is hooking up?'
- Ask about the terms 'fuck buddies' and 'friends with benefits' (FWB) – 'How do you think an FWB relationship might be selfish?' or 'How could one party

in an FWB relationship be afraid to admit to being hurt or wanting more commitment?'

- Talk about how a partner largely ignoring you in public but paying you attention in private for the sake of gaining sexual favours is not love. It is being used.
- Tell teens about far-fetched sexual stories people told you when you were young (this normalises that it is not limited to their generation).
- Explain that most girls *and guys* desire human connection and experience anxiety about romantic relationships.
- Talk about how there are many boys working really hard at becoming men of integrity. This is something young people need to hear.
- Talk about media messages about multiple sexual partners without consequence in current TV and reality shows.
- Explain that having lots of sexual partners in a month or year does not fulfil you or make you a better lover/sexual partner.
- Having had sex with one person will not assure you of the sexual needs or preferences of another person. Every person is different.
- Sex does not define you or make you a better person.

Naked selfies ('sexting')

Young people don't talk about 'sexts', they use more descriptive terms like dirty pics, n00dz, sexy texts, dick pics, etc. It is also important to keep in mind that 'sexting' (the sending of provocative sexual messages, images or videos), like sex, is not practised by all young people. We know that sexting is a complex social issue for youth, and it needs to be addressed as part of sex education and digital citizenship. Yet how we frame our conversations around sexting is vital. I'm not saying we shouldn't talk about the potential for hurt or abuse, but condemnatory language alone, rather than engaging in discussion, prevents young people from feeling comfortable enough to talk about what they or their peers are doing. This reduces our ability to help and support them when something goes wrong. The main motivations for some young people sexting include:[5]

- To demonstrate the desire to hook up.
- For approval and acceptance.
- To gain the recipient's attention.
- To control conditions and how much a recipient sees.
- To be 'flirtatious' and 'feel sexy'.
- To get the recipient to like them.
- As a 'sexy present'.
- Due to pressure from the recipient.
- To experiment with sexuality and identity.
- To show intimacy and trust with someone they are already in a relationship with.
- Yet, 81.5 per cent of girls in another survey believe it is not okay for a boyfriend to ask for nudes.[6]

Although estimates of sexting trends, among young people, vary widely, because of the differences in definitions and other factors such as age, gender or sexual identity, some small Australian studies in 2014[7] and 2015[8], both found that more young adolescents report receiving a sexually explicit message, than sending one. However, it's not difficult to see how a larger proportion of teens have received a nude. All it takes is one teen to forward a naked image to a group chat and half the class could have it by the end of lunch.

A helpful place to look for international trends on teen sexting is the 2018 meta-analysis[9] (a meta-analysis is regarded as the 'gold standard' of evidence). It found, among the 39 studies with 110380 participants, the mean prevalence for sending a sext was 14.8 percent and 27.4 percent receiving them, with rates increasing in recent years and as youth age. These percentages increase among sexually active youth. In particular, for sexually active older teens and young adults, sexting appears to be part of a sexual relationship. In addition, around 12 per cent forward sexts without consent and 8.4 per cent have them forwarded without consent. It is this non-consensual exchange that is of great concern to me. But what this data does tell us is that not everyone is sexting.

The attitudes of underage kids and sexting also vary:[10]

- The majority of young people believe (underage) sexting would hurt friendships, hurt one's chances of getting a job, would hurt romantic relationships, and would hurt relationships with your family.
- Boys are less likely to say that they would report sexting to authorities, and less likely to say that they would talk to their friends in order to prevent them from sexting.
- Boys and older youth holding more favourable attitudes toward sexting than girls and younger youth.
- Overall, girls were more likely than boys to feel that sexting would have negative consequences.

While some encourage teens to send naked selfies as sexual empowerment and self-expression (mentioned in Conversation #10), there are significant dangers with sexting and young people, including trickery, betrayal, blackmail, revenge porn, sexual predation, images ending up on porn sites and damage to a young person's reputation. Evident in the above findings is the extremely concerning fact that many young people have their images forwarded without their consent.[11] Equally worrying to me are the studies reporting girls being pressured or coerced into sending 'sexy pics'[12] then threatened if they don't comply.[13]

I have counselled a number of young people over the years, usually girls, who suffer a sense of shame because their once-private naked images followed them around. This might lead to teasing, the girls being unfairly labelled a slut, development of anxiety and occasionally engaging in self-harm. By the time I see the teens, some are on to their second or third school.

As an Ambassador for International Justice Mission, I am aware of the growing epidemic of the Online Sexual Exploitation of Children (OSEC), in which live videos and images of children are traded between countries.[14] Westerners are part of the increasing number of buyers for this abuse. This is a dark trend. While I do not support the prosecution of young people for the sometimes thoughtless impulsive decision to send or forward a naked image, celebrating or condoning it as teen sexual exploration of and experimentation with their emerging sexuality is also dangerous. I say this not to create hysteria, only to highlight the very real risks our young people face.

Ask questions that encourage critical thinking about the taking, sending and receiving of sexual images:

- 'I hope you know that if someone sends you a naked selfie and you feel uncomfortable about it, you can come and chat with me? I will never blame you or be angry with you.'
- 'What would you do with a sex video sent to you by someone else?'
- 'Do you understand why it is important that you delete the image or video immediately, and to never ever send it on to someone else?'
- 'How do you think you could respond if someone kept pressuring you to send them a naked selfie?'
- 'Do you think sending sexy pics to be flirtatious can sometimes be selfish? Why?/Why not?'

- 'Do you think there are boys who don't want or expect dirty pics? Why do you believe that?'
- 'Do you think pressuring someone for a naked selfie is okay? Why?/Why not? What if it's someone you're in a relationship with?'
- 'How do you know you can trust someone not to share a naked image you've sent them, after a break-up?'
- 'Do you think girls are blamed more than boys when a sexy image is shared around? Why do you think this is?'
- 'What do you think should be done if you find out someone at school is showing/sending dick pics around?'

Raisingchildren.net.au has further advice for parents on talking about sexting. I know from my work as a high-school teacher and school counsellor that the middle teen years are an incredibly tumultuous stage for friendships and relationships. Young people are trying to figure out so much – how to communicate well with friends, how to have a conversation with their love interest, what they enjoy, whether they agree with their parents' values, what their own values are. If we explain to teens they don't *have to* say yes to sex, that not everyone is hooking up or 'doing it', then we'll get rid of unnecessary shame, take the pressure off and allow teens to feel they can get on with the job of self-discovery and ethical growth.

Key Messages

- The incidence of hook-up culture and casual sex is greatly overestimated: most teens prefer to think about sex in the context of a serious relationship.
- Sexting is a complex social issue among youth and must be addressed as part of sex education and digital citizenship.

Misogyny and Harassment: 'Rape "jokes" are never funny.'

Not to speak is to speak, not to act is to act.

– Dietrich Bonhoeffer, anti-Nazi dissident (1905–45)

The sickness of misogyny and sexual harassment in our culture is under the spotlight more than ever – and it's about time! Of late we have seen more and more stories in the media about celebrity abuse and harassment. Some people still like to believe, however, that harassment is mainly an issue among the rich and famous, or the very poor – something that happens to 'other people' – and is not happening in their backyard. But Hollywood is like a mirror: it reflects our culture back to us, and the reflection is pretty broken right now.

And it's not just a 'grown-up' problem. This was never more clear to me than the day I sent my young teen daughter off to the beach with her friends (without an adult) for the first time. The girls had to catch a train and a ferry, and planned to be at the beach all day. After dropping her at the station, I came home angry. My then 16-year-old son and his best mate were at home and I asked them, 'Did I ever give you a rundown of being wary of public toilets, staying in groups when buying food and looking out for each other on public transport when you went to the beach on your own for the first time?' The boys said, 'No. You just told us to be sensible and call if we needed you.' I told them how I had just had to talk to my daughter about being safe from harassment. They nodded, as if it were obvious, and then a look of deep understanding filled their eyes. How different it is for boys and girls!

Harassment is extremely common in young people's lives and teens are deeply troubled by it. Obviously, porn itself is steeped in abuse, harassment and messages of misogyny, but harassment is also normalised in the everyday music and media teens consume. The more worrying trend is that it occurs at dizzying frequency in school classrooms and corridors, as well as in tertiary education settings.[1]

Many adults are so desensitised to harassment that very little has been done to address it. We have been so lulled into a sense of normalcy that research has found that by the end of preschool, children already start segregating and stereotyping by sex. By the time they finish high school, a shocking 87 per cent of women (in a survey[2] of 18- to 25-year-olds) report having endured at least one form of harassment, and another[3] found that 81 per cent of women have experienced harassment at some point in their lives. The forms of harassment include being touched without permission by a stranger, insulted with sexualised words, having a stranger say something sexual to them and having a stranger 'catcall' or tell them they were 'hot'. Girls I talk to tell me how upsetting it is when they have someone come and 'grind' on them from behind at a party and then walk away, being cheered by mates.

The effects

Sexual harassment and abuse cause damage to romantic relationships and many other areas of young people's lives. Misogyny can lead to lasting fears and shame in girls. It destroys wellbeing and holds them back in school and later in the workforce. In addition, young men's and boys' capacity to have meaningful relationships with both men and women is eroded over time.

What teens need

Significant numbers of young people report never having had a conversation with a parent about what sexual harassment is. They have never been helped with what they should do if they experience sexual harassment or how to avoid sexually harassing others. They have not had a conversation about not catcalling or not making degrading comments about girls. Despite the fact that one in five women report being sexually assaulted during college in the US, most of the respondents to the above survey had never spoken with their parents about sexual pressure or harassment.

Teens need more adults to step up and help them. They need to know what it means to care for people of different genders, as well as to understand what care and respect look like, in and out of a sexual context. (See the conversations on emotional intelligence, objectification and sex education for more on this.)

What can we do?

1. **Start teaching equality in preschool.** It has been found that children who are encouraged to play with friends of the opposite sex learn better problem-solving and communication skills. In addition, boys who have friendships with girls are less likely to think of women as sexual conquests as they grow up.

Here is an example of teaching sons to think of girls as people, by Megan Powell-Du Toit, a Sydney teacher, pastor and mother of two boys. This was on her Facebook page and later expanded on in a blog post:

*Parents of teenage girls. Many of you my friends. I hear
your worries and fears. I'm the mother of a teen boy and
an almost teen boy. I'm accepting my responsibility to
help change this #metoo world through bringing up boys
who respect girls.*

> *Here's what I am trying to teach them:*
> *It isn't your business what a girl wears.*
> *She doesn't owe you attention.*
> *Ask before you hug, kiss or go further.*
> *You are responsible for your own actions.*
> *Girls are equal to you.*
> *But they don't experience an equal world.*
> *Listen to their experiences.*
> *Stand up for them.*
> *Do what you can to help them stay safe.*
> *Girls make awesome friends.*
> *Be an awesome friend back to them.*
> *I do this not just for your girls but for my boys. This
> is part of learning how to have good relationships.*

*Two further comments. Firstly, in this, I'm not
negating the need to teach sexual morality to our kids.
Instead, I am adding an essential principle of respect
for women that has often been missing or underplayed.
Secondly, all of the points I mentioned above need
expanding. We need to teach our kids the context and
practice of each point, developing each further as they
get older. They also need modelling. Especially by adult
men around these kids. So dads, uncles, pastors and
youth leaders, please, show us how it is done.*

**2. Teach young people to identify common forms of misogyny
and harassment.** These can be so ingrained into social norms
that they don't immediately recognise them in their peer groups.
Highlight catcalling or using gender-based slurs ('bitch', 'whore',

'slut') as part of misogynistic culture, and clearly describe what kind of behaviour constitutes harassment. As an example and explained by my friend Cailtin Roper (a feminist writer and activist against the sexualisation of women and girls) the terms 'slut' and 'whore' are increasingly used by boys and girls, as gendered slurs to demean girls. These terms are deeply rooted in misogyny and serve to diminish the humanity of women and girls. Girls can be called sluts despite having done nothing to warrant the label, or even simply for rejecting boys' sexual advances. The term slut is often applied indiscriminately to women and girls to keep them in their place. The act of branding a girl a slut or a whore dehumanises her. It sends the message that she is different from other girls – lesser somehow. She is viewed as deserving of ridicule, contempt or even sexual violence. When a girl is a 'slut', this communicates that it is appropriate for boys to demean and treat her like an object.

3. Call out rape 'jokes' and 'rape culture' in memes, T-shirt slogans and music lyrics among teens and their peers (and even adults). Call out terms like 'I hit that', 'I nailed that', 'We really raped that team'. Don't stay silent – insist that these phrases are never funny, and that bonding over the dehumanisation of another person is completely unacceptable. Ask questions like, 'How did this become a way for you and your friends to joke and bond?' 'How did the dehumanisation of a woman become a fashion statement?' Explain how 'jokes' and music lyrics seep into the way we think and normalise how we act towards others. Join activist movements that hold companies and celebrities to account.

4. Step in when you witness misogyny and harassment – too many parents stay silent when it happens. This speaks volumes about what we believe. Sometimes we freeze because we don't know what to say, but being passive leads teens to believe we condone the comments and also diminishes young people's respect for the adults in their lives. Encourage your sons and daughters to call out harassment if they are in a group (for safety's sake), or to go to the aid of a victim by sitting next to them on public transport, or by walking them home. Brainstorm ways that they can also remain personally safe in these situations. theline.org.au provides many practical examples for young people in addressing everyday misogyny and harassment:[4]

- **Address the comment, not the person**
  'Nobody likes hearing that ...'
  'That's pretty offensive if you think about it ...'
- **Ask a question that makes them rethink their statement**
  'How do you think that makes them feel?'
  'I don't get it – what does that mean ...?'
- **Use a 'we statement' to gain support from people around you**
  'Yeah, I'm not sure we'd all agree with you there ...'
  'Is it just me or does everyone here think that's out of line?'
- **Make the connection between the comment and the person's own experience**
  'So, would you say that about your girlfriend/sister/ mother?'
  'How do you reckon your girlfriend/sister/mother feels when people say stuff like that?'
- **Take non-verbal action**
  If you really don't feel comfortable speaking up sometimes, you can just give 'a look' to make it clear you thought the comment was lame. Don't laugh – just sigh, shake your head, or walk away.
  If you're not up for saying something at the time, you can always let someone know afterwards – in a less public space, where you're both more comfortable – that

*you don't rate what they're saying. Remember, people
can get defensive and you don't need to get into an
argument – just state your case and ask them if they can
see your perspective.*

5. Be understanding if your teen says they have witnessed
harassment and been too afraid to stand up to it. Ask what might
stop them from intervening in situations. Acknowledge that the
dynamics of a situation can be tricky. Help your teen to think of
ways they can support a victim in getting help after an incident.

6. Ask if your teen has ever been harassed or insulted with
sexualised words or behaviours, and how they responded. If
it has happened to them, ask if they would like to talk about
it with you or a counsellor. Ask if they would feel comfortable
confronting the person harassing them, with someone there to
support them.

7. If they have not been harassed, brainstorm ways of
responding in various situations, should it happen to them or a
friend.

8. Emphasise that it is never okay to touch anyone without their
permission.

9. Talk about sexual assault. No one wants to talk about rape.
Parents don't want to think that their son could be guilty of ever
raping someone. Yet, in truth, many boys (and girls) still hold
some really outdated – and completely wrong – ideas about girls
and sex. We need to debunk these erroneous ideas with teens:
  - If she dresses in a certain way, she must want sex.
  - If I spoil her and spend money on her, she owes me sex.
  - If she is flirty, she must want sex.
  - If she doesn't say no, it means she wants sex.

10. Talk about the rape myth. The 'rape myth' normalises blaming the victim rather than the perpetrator. That is, if a girl says something, dresses or acts in a certain way, she must have asked to be raped, or it must somehow be her fault. Talk about how old ladies and women in nun's habits or hijabs get raped too. Talk about the blame being solely on the part of the abuser and his need for power. (Please see the conversations on love and sex education for more on this.)

Key Messages

- Teach your children from a young age that girls and boys are equal, and that misogyny and harassment are never okay.
- Help them identify harassment in their everyday lives and brainstorm ways they can combat it.
- Join activist movements that hold companies and celebrities to account.

Pornography: 'We need to talk about porn.'

What we are witnessing is an unprecedented experiment on the sexual development of children. Our kids are growing up in a shadow cast by pornography. The big difference now is that it comes to them at the click of a button. They don't even have to go looking for porn – porn will find them.

– Melinda Tankard Reist, activist and author, Collective Shout

After one of my seminars, a mum came up to me, distressed. She knew my topic was going to be on porn culture and so she was curious about what her boys (ages 10 and 11) knew about it. She assumed she was getting in really early with them on the topic, as they had never brought it up at home and went to what she believed to be a 'good school'. She had also made sure they had blocking software, which prevents access to certain websites, installed on their devices from an early age. She was completely unprepared for the fact that her boys had already heard about porn, having been exposed to conversations and some images through their mates at soccer the season before. They hadn't brought it up because they were both embarrassed and afraid. The brothers didn't know how to talk about it and assumed their parents didn't think they should, because it had never been mentioned at home. They were also scared that their parents would ban them from technology.

It's not just boys. Another mother came to talk with me after one of my seminars and thanked me for mentioning that accessing pornography was not just a 'boy issue'. She told me about her friend's 9-year-old girl, who was in therapy and struggling with depression because she had been secretly watching porn for six months. Her mum had installed blocking software on her older brothers' devices, but had assumed her daughter was too young to stumble upon inappropriate content – she was just watching cartoons, or so the mother thought. These are the kinds of conversations I have with parents both in counselling sessions and after each parenting seminar, every single week.

These mothers' stories are not isolated incidents: they tie in to the report by ChildLine in the UK, which indicates one-third of their 11 000 counselling sessions about online issues specifically related to online sexual abuse (viewing sexually explicit content, sharing sexual images and online child sexual exploitation).[1] This was also a 60 per cent increase in counselling sessions being offered in 2016–17, compared to the previous period. Many young people reported being reluctant to tell anyone about their online experience because they were worried about their parents finding out what they had been doing online, or felt they were to blame. As the stories of the mums at my seminars illustrate, these stats are real people. They are the children and teens I know and work with.

Like these mums discovered, the flood of porn is available to our children as a primary source of sex education.[2] If not specifically addressed, it is likely to erode the work we have put into other conversations we've had. Porn has the ability to destroy everything that is good about romance, love and relationships – there is nothing empathic or kind about porn.[3] Hence, the issue of porn absolutely must be part of our conversations with our young people.[4]

These stories aren't meant to scare you. As I said, this is a book about hope, and hope needs always to be greater than the problem, otherwise we will crumble under the problem's weight. But as with any enemy, particularly one that wishes to devour our children, we must not be caught sleeping! We need to know what it is capable of, so we know how to face it.

So, please, parents – *please* – don't ever say, 'Not my child.' The minute you allow yourself to say that, you put your child at risk. Rather, say to yourself, 'I know it will happen, it's just a matter of *when* – and I will be ready and armed.'

The impacts of pornography on young people

This is a public health crisis. Like smoking or other public health issues, this will have long-term consequences.

– Dr Joe Tucci, CEO, Australian Childhood Foundation

I was a speaker at the National Pornography Harms Children and Young People Symposium, hosted by eChildhood at Sydney University in 2016 and the Society for the Advancement of Sexual Health conference in the USA in 2018. At each conference, a range of academics, child development experts and advocates addressed porn as a public health crisis. The general consensus is that the nature of contemporary mainstream pornography does not in any way resemble the images today's adults may have been exposed to when they were young. When I talk with parents about pornography, I refer to the parent naiveté gap. Pornography is not simply a few naked breasts or a couple of people having intercourse.

One of the reasons why pornography is generally overlooked as a sexual health issue is the generation gap created by internet pornography. The term pornography generally

*conjures up images of a pizza delivery guy arriving at the
house of a sexually aroused housewife or girl next door.
However, the internet has significantly reshaped the content
of pornography. Now, the most popular and easily accessible
forms of pornography contain significant amounts of violence,
degradation and humiliation of women, are short, and focused
almost exclusively on genitalia. Many adults, who are beyond
the years of sexual development and exploration and who
developed their sexual identities prior to the internet, have not
encountered the new sexual scripts. Internet pornography is
inscribing on the sexual identities of younger people.*

– Australian Psychological Society,[5] 2016

Areas of pornography's negative impact and effects on children and young people include:

- Increased rates of exposure in children.[6]
- Age of first exposure being generally lower in boys than in girls, with more boys than girls viewing online porn by choice.[7, 8]
- Young people more likely than not to have seen online pornography by the time they are 15, with almost half of boys seeing porn before 13.[9, 10, 11]
- Seeing porn websites when they did not intend to access them, with 45 per cent in one study reporting being 'very' or 'somewhat' upset by it.[12, 13]
- Adolescents being considered one of the most susceptible audiences to the messages portrayed in porn.[14, 15]
- Negative feelings (shock, curiosity, confusion) subsiding through repeated viewing of online pornography.[16]
- Encouragement of underage sexual activity.[17]
- A rise in child-on-child sexual offences and increase in numbers of children in treatment for Problem Sexualised Behaviours (PSBs).[18, 19, 20]
- Insecurities about sexual performance and body image.[21, 22]

- Links between emotional and mental health issues and problematic porn use.[23, 24, 25, 26]
- Higher pornography use leads to less enjoyment of sexually intimate behaviours with a real-life partner.[27]
- Growing evidence of a link between problematic pornography use and the rise in reports of low sexual desire and erectile dysfunction in young men and high schoolers.[28]
- Growing evidence of a link between problematic pornography use and the rise in reports of low sexual desire and erectile dysfunction in young men and high schoolers[29]
- Viewing casual sex, without affection or relationship, as the norm.[30]
- Cynicism about love and perceptions of exaggerated sexual activity in society.[31]
- Shaping sexual behaviours through belief in the pornographic script, i.e., expectations of what is deemed 'appropriate sex'.[32, 33]
- Willingness to 'try out' what is shown in porn and engage in more casual sex.[34, 35]
- Increased sexual risk taking, such as unsafe practices, and more sexual partners.[36, 37]
- Normalised coercive, painful and unsafe anal heterosex.[38]
- Coercive sexual bullying, sexual aggression and forced sex among young people who consumed pornography.[39, 40, 41]
- Sexism and objectification training in both boys and girls.[42, 43, 44]
- Reinforcement of the 'rape myth'.[45, 46]
- Increasing evidence that internet porn use may cause addiction-related brain changes.[47, 48, 49]

For a comprehensive analysis of the research, not-for-profit eChildhood's statement of research can be found on their website.[50]

What can we do?

Children and teens are curious about their bodies, their
development and sex. I've already mentioned that neither sex nor
sexual attraction is inherently bad – it is part of normal, healthy
development. We ought to be encouraging young people to be safe,
healthy and confident about their bodies and sexual development.
The problem is that the sexualised wallpaper of society does not
allow for this natural development to occur. With pornography as
a major influence in their lives, children are forced into an early
awareness of unhealthy and even dangerous sexual practices.[51]
Young people have questions, and although an Irish survey[52] found
most young people feel comfortable talking to their peers about
sex, their peers are tuning in to the same broken sources they are.
Young people need strong alternative voices to those of Pornland.

Something we need to be keenly aware of is that children often
don't tell adults when they have seen pornography, because they
fear having their technology taken away. Which is why we need
to be talking to our younger children about content they might be
exposed to, *before it happens*. We need to reassure them that when
they come and talk to us about something they have seen, we will
not be angry and will not suddenly ban them from their screens.
We could say something like, 'Sometimes there may be pictures
you are shown, or which you click on, that are upsetting, make you
feel sick in your tummy or which you think are inappropriate. You
can always come and tell me about them. In fact, I hope you do.
I will not be angry with you and I won't suddenly take away your
device. In fact, I will be proud of you, that you are brave enough
to come and talk to me about it.' For young children, the picture
books, *Good Pictures Bad Pictures* by Kristen A. Jenson and Gail
Poyner, and *Not for Kids!* by Liz Walker for Protecting Kids Online
are helpful resources for parents wanting to start this discussion.

Conversations with tweens and teens can be even more specific.

Although I have already mentioned that most young people
want to hear more from adults about sex and relationships, many

still feel uncomfortable talking about this with their parents.[53] I believe this might be because parents don't make this a normal part of their conversations, so kids will not be the ones to bring it up first.

The encouraging news is that a strong parent–child attachment is highly associated with teens avoiding risky online behaviours. The research says that teens who reported strong relationships with their parents were less likely to experience problematic internet use, view pornography or participate in sexting.[54] This emphasises the importance of parents nurturing a strong relationship with their children.

Parents – you matter a great deal!

Porn as a poisonous script vs lessons in intimacy (a topic for teens)

Whenever I talk with teens about the effects of porn, I mention the idea that porn has hijacked our sexuality – it serves as a script for sexual behaviour. So rather than one day growing up and discovering what they enjoy or don't enjoy in a sexual relationship, porn bullies teen into thinking about sex in toxic, stereotypical ways. Rather than learning about intimacy and emotion, or figuring out their own or their eventual partner's needs, desires and preferences, porn teaches what they 'should do', 'should want' and 'should enjoy', long before many teens have even had their first kiss. In my talks for teens, I tell them that when they watch porn, they get sold lies. I highlight that porn is a counterfeit of real intimacy and relationships. It is not how healthy and loving relationships work.

Use online videos as conversation starters with young teens. As an example, I currently use videos by Fight the New Drug and 'Russell Brand Talks Sex, Softcore and Hardcore Porn' when I talk with teens about the damage porn inflicts upon our hearts, minds and relationships. I tell teens that, via porn, they learn:

- This is what sex is.

- This is what girls want.
- This is what sexually attractive bodies *should* look like.
- This is what we *should* look like while having sex.
- This is what we *should* enjoy in a sexual encounter.
- Everyone *must* be having sex, and I am odd if I choose not to.

Teens need to hear that just because someone has watched porn, it does not mean that they are going to be great in bed. What they are seeing in porn is staged, often abusive, and is not healthy sex. It lacks healthy reciprocity. In actual fact, porn serves as a manual for becoming a bad lover because it is a very poor sex educator. Porn sex is broken sex.

They need to hear the messages in Conversation #10: sex is about *more* than tricks and secret techniques. Good sex is about *both* parties working together, and that requires being able to actually talk, to understand and *be* understood. Sexual intimacy requires honesty, openness, self-disclosure and even confiding concerns and fears. It is thinking about the other person, not just about yourself.

Because young people *do* think about what is important in their relationships, they will be open to hearing that porn is the opposite of a healthy relationship. That is, one of mutual respect, friendship and humour.

Your body's response is normal

Teens need to hear that sexual thoughts and feelings happen as part of normal development. However, it's what they choose to do with those feelings or thoughts that matters. Also, that 'normal' is different for every person and every relationship – which is why honest communication is important. So when they do eventually enter a committed relationship that involves sex, what is normal and pleasing needs to work for both parties.

It is vital for teens to hear that people respond to their first exposure to pornography differently too. Sexologist Liz

Walker refers to 'normal' responses to exposure as a range that includes curiosity, revulsion, confusion, shame, guilt, arousal, or compulsion. She believes that for some teens to be curious or even aroused when first encountering pornography is their body's natural inbuilt physiological responses; it is the way we are designed. However, it's what we choose to do after our first encounters with pornography that puts us onto a healthy or destructive path. Do you continue to look for more and more opportunities to watch porn? Do you tell a trusted friend or adult about it, do you make a decision that this is not the type of sexual content you want to begin to shape your life? This is why it is so important for young people to have someone to talk with when they first encounter porn – someone who does not magnify the guilt and shame, which often leads porn viewing to become a secretive, and potentially more compulsive behaviour.

Pornland sex contains distorted messages

Teens don't know that much of porn is violent and abusive, yet this is portrayed as okay and even enjoyable in porn scenes. Porn is filled with myths and stereotypes – whether it's about gender roles, race or penis size (even body parts are disproportionate and often surgically enhanced for porn scenes). Pornland sex normalises a power imbalance, because in real life young women don't want to be physically and mentally humiliated, as portrayed in pornography.

Pornography normalises treating people as objects

This is where discussions about the porn industry being a multi-billion-dollar industry need to happen. Teens need to hear that the industry doesn't care about people. That the industry itself is abusive and supports the objectification of women and children, and that much of what is shown contains nonconsensual sex and helps fuel the sex trade. We should also talk about how viewing porn is a form of sexual objectification (i.e using others' bodies for our own sexual pleasure). And as adults, we need to model our own everyday choices, in what we watch and how we view others.

Negative biological and psychological effects

Talk to teens about the growing evidence that links compulsive porn viewing with changes in their brain structure. Teen boys I speak with often respond with shock when they hear that there is mounting evidence that compulsive porn users are increasingly seeking help for issues with erectile dysfunction, and that many people with problematic pornography use struggle to have an intimate relationship with a real person.

What do I do when I discover my child has seen porn?

If we talk with our children about the harms of pornography, does that mean they will never see it or even seek it out? Unfortunately, no! We've already ascertained that they *will* see porn, sooner than we feel prepared for – children are curious and porn is everywhere. But we are in this for the long haul. We are obligated to inform our children of the grave risks they face if they choose porn. We have to teach them not just the biological truths, but also about their own emotional vulnerabilities and to value the highest standard of care for others. Again – one big talk is not enough! We will be having lots of small talks on various topics, at every age, stage and level of exposure.

When it happens – **BREATHE**:

> **B**e ready
> **R**eassure
> **E**xpect initial denials or promises
> **A**ctivities
> **T**echnology check
> **H**ave a plan
> **E**nlist support

Be ready

No matter how prepared you think you are to talk about this, when it infiltrates your own family *you never feel ready*. It is natural for parents to want to protect their children from harm, and most parents I speak to believe porn is harmful to their children. So when you find out your child's innocence has been stolen too soon, you might be furious and shocked and sick to your stomach – and you ought to be, but not at your child. Never at your child! Your child is terrified and confused and overwhelmed enough already, without having guilt added to their trauma. When pornography first came into my home I went and sat in the pantry to gather my thoughts. Yes, I'm serious! (And keep in mind that I talk about the problem of porn for a living.) Even I wasn't ready for all the stats to come slamming into my kitchen at that moment. Because those stats were now my own children, and I mourned the fact. Of course I knew it would happen – but I still hated that it had, because I'm their mum. I needed to ensure that my response to this discovery did not cause my child to feel further shame or rejection.

So, be ready. If being ready means you read everything you can about the harmful consequences of pornography, then do that. If being ready means you read and reread this chapter, then do that. If being ready means talking to other parents, then do that. And if being ready means that when porn comes into your child's life, you go and hide in the pantry to regroup and think about what you want to say first, and take a few moments to *breathe* – then do *that*! Take a little time before responding. Don't jump straight in and blurt out your fears and concerns. Go for a walk, if necessary, to calm yourself down and think about what you might say next. Then, be ready to talk.

Reassure

I know of one teen boy who sobbed when his mum found him watching porn. He said, 'You will never look at me the same again.' His mum did a great job of reassuring and caring for him.

Tell your child what you found or noticed. Ask kindly what happened and tell them you are sorry they have been dealing with this alone. Again: refrain from sounding judgemental, no matter what you find. Don't punish and yell or tell your child how 'bad' they now are. They need to hear that they are not dirty or evil. Tell them you love them, and no matter what they do, you will never stop loving them. They need to be reassured that you care about the person they become, which is why you want to talk about this even more, now and into the future. Reassure them that you will not take away all technology. Tell them the good news: that their age counts in their favour, because they can develop good habits when they're put in place early. Their brain can develop new, healthy ways of thinking and it is not too late to start afresh. Remind them that you are there for support and that many people around the world are fighting against porn. Importantly, if you haven't tackled the conversation well the first time, apologise! Tell your child you are angry at the pornographers and people who exploit women and children for profit. Emphasise to your child that it came out all wrong, that you love them and you would like to start the conversation over.

Expect initial denials or promises

Expect denials from your child that they actually saw the porn, or sought it out. Expect promises that it wasn't theirs or it just popped up accidentally (this might occasionally be the case – especially in young children), but the denials usually come from confusion, shame and embarrassment. They know it's somehow not right. Expect your child to promise that they will *never* look at it again. At the time they might genuinely mean this; however, many will – some out of curiosity, some because they will have it sent to them by others and some out of compulsion – even though they don't wish to. Talk about this and reassure your child using some of the points I covered in 'What can we do?', which begins on page 204.

Activities

Ensure your child's life is filled with other fun and engaging activities, those that develop self-confidence and self-worth and alleviate boredom. We can't simply stop doing something, without replacing it with something else. A void must always be filled, otherwise we just go back to old habits. Activities also create the need to have a routine, and healthy routines allow for development of new self-disciplines.

Technology check

Ideally we would have age restrictions set up for apps, movie accounts like Netflix and games already, but a child's exposure to pornography can often jolt parents into doing this for the first time, or checking the device settings again. If not done already, add filtering software and check age-restriction settings for apps, TV, movies and websites, on all devices. Children under 13 should not be on social media (parents are often shocked to find out how much porn is easily available on Instagram and even YouTube).

Most devices have a parental control setting that will need your password before restrictions can be adjusted. There are plenty of websites that provide parents with a step-by-step guide to setting these up (see Online Support on page 217). Yet I am still astounded at the number of households that have no blocking or filtering software on devices, and how rarely parents check on their child's social media activities[55, 56] – even homes where pornography has been found on children's devices. Parents naively think exposure is a one-off occurrence and believe their children won't seek it out again.

Parents should do occasional content spot-checks and know their children's and younger teens' passwords – not in a snoopy or stalky way, rather as part of healthy boundaries and caring for your children's wellbeing. If you start this off openly and when they get their first devices, it will become quite normal in your family. I encourage parents to think of their child's device the same way they would swimming pools and cars. We don't throw our little children into pools and hope they will stay afloat: we take them to swimming lessons – often for years before they are proficient. Even teens need a fully licensed driver sitting beside them for a full year before being allowed onto the roads on their own. Yet somehow we simply hand over devices with full access to the online world without a thought or restriction in place. It is our job to set boundaries and train our children to handle the virtual highway responsibly.

Most importantly, *ensure that technology is out of bedrooms at night!* (Remember: porn is accessed on smartphones too.) Every device should be plugged in at a family charging dock at bedtimes. However, there is no software that is completely failsafe. As an example, filtering software is not yet advanced enough to detect images and videos uploaded to social media sites. These can only be taken down if reported by a user. So a content check-in needs to form part of a broader plan (see below).

Finally, encourage your children to fill their online world with positive alternatives to sexualisation and pornography.

Have a plan

Technology boundaries, healthy activities and ongoing support need to be intentionally thought through, and formulated into a plan for healthy lifestyles and safe technology use.

My 'Support Triad' forms part of helping families develop a plan, and I have begun using it increasingly in my talks with parents and schools. Young people need a healthy support plan to fall back on in times of need or distress (and not just when confronted with porn), because trying to come up with healthy alternatives in 'the heat of the moment' is rarely successful.

The Support Triad can be discussed or completed as a written activity with kids and teens, but must be paired with technology boundaries and filtering software.

The following options will change with age and stage, but get your child to list:

- Three safe people they can turn to, call up or contact if they need support or help (at least two out of three should be adults). And please be okay with the fact that sometimes these people may not always include a parent. Safe adults might include Grandma, an adult cousin, a youth leader, a friend's mum, a teacher or a coach.
- Three safe activities – these should be life giving, healthy and enjoyable. Things that take their minds off destructive activities and fill the void. They could include sport, hobbies, baking, or walking the dog.
- Three safe places – examples might include the garden, the park, a sports club, a friend or grandparents' home.

Three safe people

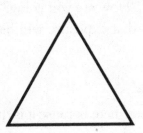

Three safe activities   Three safe places

Additionally, for a young person who has already been accessing porn, you will need to help them notice times they seek it out, because there is usually a pattern that evolves. (When Mum is still at work? When Dad pops out to drop their brother at soccer?) Help your child recognise their triggers. (When bored? When stressed? During exams? When feeling depressed or lonely? When tired?) This helps them begin to take ownership of their behaviours and helps them plan to find healthy alternatives and distractions during these times. As part of your plan use some of the conversations listed throughout this book in your follow-up chats.

Shame is a big part of why young people don't talk about their porn use and usually drives them further into secrecy. Remind your child that they can come to you about anything, no matter what they have seen or been shown, whether they've fallen off the plan or not – you will work out what to do together.

Enlist support

Tell your child that if they don't feel they can talk with you about their questions or concerns about porn, it is important they have another trusted adult they can talk with. Then figure out together who this person might be (a grandparent, an aunt, a school counsellor). Let them know that it will become easier once they get used to new habits and ways of thinking, but that it is important to always have someone for support and for accountability, to ask, 'How are you going?'

As a parent know that exposure will happen again, but you will be prepared.

Porn 'addictions'

I use the term 'addiction' here because it is the word we all readily recognise when something becomes compulsive and begins to affect your life in negative ways, but this is not the official terminology. Problematic Pornography Use (or pornography 'addiction') would fall under what is referred to as 'compulsive sexual behaviour disorder' in the World Health Organization's recently updated ICD-11 (the ICD-11 stands for International

Classification of Diseases – version 11). Simply, this is an international standard for reporting medical and psychological conditions used in more than 100 countries around the world.

As with any addiction, only a small amount of the population would fit the criteria for a full blown pornography addiction. However, if anything is affecting a young person's life in negative ways, this must be taken seriously, and we must get them the help they need.

What are the 6 factors for determining problematic pornography use?[57]:

- Salience – how prominent pornography viewing has become in a person's life.
- Mood modification – where pornography is used to release tension, negative feelings, or restore feelings of tranquillity.
- Conflict – when porn viewing leads to negative life consequences, due to the compulsive habit which might include; ruined relationships, trouble at school (or work), loss of interest in nonsexual activities, shame, depression, anxiety, loss of community standing, legal issues, financial problems, and others.
- Tolerance – needing to watch more porn, or more 'extreme' versions of porn to gain satisfaction/arousal.
- Relapse – a number of failed attempts to stop or cut back the amount of porn watched, despite vowing to do so.
- Withdrawal – experiencing distress or agitation or 'missing' porn when unable to watch it.

If you realise that pornography viewing has become problematic, please do not shame your child, because shame already drives this self-destructive behaviour. Further shame can cause them to continue the behaviour in secret and spiral deeper into an addiction cycle. Shame leads a child to believe 'I am bad' compared to 'my habit or choice is bad'. Shame is different from guilt: shame comes from a feeling of 'badness' about the self, whereas guilt is about a behaviour. Guilt comes from a feeling of 'conscience' about the bad choices you have made, which go against your values. Of course, helping young people to make new healthy choices is a vital part of the recovery process, but it is very difficult to believe you can change your behaviours if you are full of shame and believe there is no hope for you.

As a start, use my steps above, but ask your child kindly if there are other steps you might take together to help them get the compulsion under control. Getting your child on board with this is very important – wanting to stop needs to come from them also. But there may be times parents need to step in with firmer boundaries, to help a young person who does not yet recognise how bad their habit has become.

Seeking support from a psychologist is usually vital at this stage, as there can often be other issues that co-exist, such as depression, social anxiety, and impulse control problems. For some, it can also be used as a form of self-medication, in the same way that teens use alcohol or drugs to numb or escape their underlying issues. Although, Problematic Pornography Use does not always come out of a child having other issues. It sometimes develops into a destructive compulsion, after initially starting out as curiosity.

A child cannot make the necessary changes with a therapist on their own. Parents must be involved, by supporting the young person and helping them to implement any of the household or behaviour changes the therapist might suggest.

Your child may need to learn how to form healthy social bonds and relearn how to connect in healthy ways. Long-term accountability is recognised as one of the most effective ways of maintaining control over the addiction.

When teens are at risk in this area, it is also strongly recommended that parents, with the support of a psychologist, closely monitor online activity and severely limit access to pornography on file-sharing networks and elsewhere. This is particularly helpful in the early stages of treatment.

The good news is that although the messages in porn can severely damage a child's understanding of relationships at a time when they are still forming their views on love and sex and intimacy, early healing can turn an isolated life into a life of joy and connection once again.

Online support

The sheer volume of websites and new games can feel overwhelming for parents to monitor. I suggest following or subscribing to websites that advise parents of new apps and games popular with children. These are websites I recommend, which alert parents to some of the dangers and often provide a step-by-step approach for creating privacy or restriction settings:

- The Cybersafety Lady thecybersafetylady.com.au
- Common Sense Media www.commonsensemedia.org
- Ask the Mediatrician cmch.tv/parents/askthemediatrician
- Australian Council on Children and the Media (ACCM) childrenandmedia.org.au
- My own website collettsmart.com

Advocacy groups you could join with, to enter the fight against the sexploitation of children and their exposure to porn, include:

- eChildhood www.echildhood.org
- Fight the New Drug fightthenewdrug.org
- Culture Reframed www.culturereframed.org
- Beauty Redefined beautyredefined.org
- Collective Shout collectiveshout.org

Key Messages

- The flood of porn is available to our children at every turn. If not specifically addressed, it is likely to erode the work we have put into other conversations we've had.
- Reinforce the idea that porn is a counterfeit of real intimacy and relationships. It is not how healthy and loving relationships work.
- When you learn your child has been exposed to porn, **BREATHE: B**e ready, **R**eassure, **E**xpect initial denials or promises, **A**ctivities, **T**echnology check, **H**ave a plan, **E**nlist support.
- Encourage your child to fill their online world with positive alternatives to sexualised and pornographic content.
- Always strive to be reassuring and supportive to maintain open communication with your child. Avoid shaming your child.

Manners and Helping: '"Thank you" and "Can I help?" vs "I want ..."'

Who can really be faithful in great things if he has not learned to be faithful in the things of daily life?
– Dietrich Bonhoeffer, anti-Nazi dissident (1905–45)

We all know a person – or two – who thinks the world owes them something. They complain and demand things from others, and just never seem content. They're unpleasant to be around. Adults don't arrive at this overnight – they are bred this way, by their parents never having expectations of them growing up. Teaching gratitude and responsibility is an inoculation against entitlement – parents who teach appreciation of others and that life is about more than ourselves and what we want in the moment set their children up to be kind and empathetic adults.

Back to basics

Inoculating kids against a selfish mindset seems so simple because it's about going back to the basics.

'Thank you!'

When children are taught to be thankful, they learn to consider the sacrifice and kindness that others have shown them. They learn that parents, siblings or friends are not there to serve their own needs. In turn, when we thank our children for their help or kindness, we teach them what it feels like to be appreciated. Practising thankfulness actually changes the structure of the brain and pulls it out of negative-thinking ruts. In particular, taking the time to record just three things that one is grateful for each day, over a 2-week period, is shown to reduce stress and increase wellbeing.[1]

TRY THIS:

Work thankfulness into daily conversations:

- Model gratitude by thanking your children when they are helpful or demonstrate kindness.
- Put love or appreciation notes into young children's lunchboxes or under your teen's pillow.
- Send appreciation texts to family members.
- Have a family 'Grateful for You Jar', where you pop in a note to each family member once a week, and then read them out once a month.
- Buy each child a personal thankfulness journal or box, or make use of a family gratitude pin board, where 3 points of gratitude can be added each day over a few weeks.
- Teach children to have a thankful heart by asking them to mention one activity, action or person they are thankful for each day (this needs to extend beyond material items). Family meals or bedtimes are often good for this.
- Encourage children to say 'thank you' to others in their lives: friends, teachers, coaches, Grandma, etc.

- Write 'thank you' letters and texts to people you are grateful to – and not just for the big things, but the everyday stuff too.

'Can I help you?'

Requiring children to help around the house, as well as volunteering in the community, is a way for them to develop gratitude and an outward-looking mindset.

Doing chores

As a society we are actually expecting less of our children around the house, to their future detriment. But adults are not the servants in the home, and children are often capable of more than their parents give them credit for. Having children be part of everyday chores creates opportunities for gratitude and helps kids realise that things take effort. Studies reveal that participation in chores from a young age is instrumental in predicting children's overall success into their mid-20s and mental wellness into late adulthood.[2] Chores lead to:

- Acknowledging the importance of contributing to their family.
- Better relationships with friends and family.
- An ability to work well with others.
- Delayed gratification: 'I can play with my toys after I have fed the dog.'
- Greater self-discipline.
- Enhanced gross and fine motor skills.
- Developing a 'pitch-in' mindset: 'Stuff needs to be done and it's up to me.'
- A sense of empathy as adults.
- Greater career success.

While making the bed or picking up toys are important, chores should be something that benefit the whole family too. Additionally, chores should not be part of pocket money, as daily tasks are simply a part of life: Mum and Dad don't get paid for making dinner or washing clothes, for example. Perhaps we could rephrase family 'chores' as family 'contributions'? Extra jobs around the house might be used for pocket money. My husband is very good at DIY, so when he decided to build a deck around the pool, rather than get someone in he asked my teens if they wanted to earn extra money and he paid them to help. They all got to be outside together and chat, and my sons and daughter learned new skills and earned extra money.

But what about the complaining?

Yes – kids will complain about doing chores. Don't you? I know I complain when I have to do the laundry! Initially, most children won't do their chores very well, because they will need some practice and guidance. Show them exactly what the chore entails and even demonstrate how to do it properly. Don't expect perfection (especially from little ones) but it's okay to call kids back if chores are done poorly. If a parent just re-does the job every time, children either get a sense that it's never good enough or that they can just do a half-job and then run off because Mum will fix it. Successfully getting your child to do chores is about finding the balance and assessing their capability.

In my home we have a whiteboard with a rotating roster, which is very helpful, so that everyone can see who does what and when. It is important, however, that the chore/contribution schedule works for you and your family routine. Having a specific time each day for contributions to be done is also helpful.

Some ideas by age:

- 2–3-year-olds can put away toys and pick up scatter cushions in the lounge room, set out their clothes for the next day, help put clean dishes away by sorting plastics, and take dirty clothes to the laundry.
- 4–5-year-olds can help feed pets, make their beds (perhaps not perfectly), help clear the table after dinner, water plants, fold small items of clothing, set part of the table, and dust.
- 6–7-year-olds can wipe tables and counters, put laundry away, prepare school snacks, and vacuum floors.
- 7–9-year-olds can load and unload the dishwasher, help prepare simple meals and make school lunches, unpack groceries, and help clean the bathroom.
- 10–11-year-olds can change their bedding, clean the kitchen or bathrooms, do laundry, and take out rubbish bags.
- Children aged 12 and above can wash the car, help shop for groceries with a list, mow the lawn, and cook a simple meal. Older teens can babysit younger siblings.

If you didn't start at a young age, just start now – it's never too late to begin a new family habit. When you wonder if it's worth it, remind yourself that you are helping your children to be more successful later in life.

The benefits of volunteering

You know the saying 'actions speak louder than words'? This is true for demonstrating thankfulness and kindness to others, because when we teach children to look outwards, their own needs and problems come into perspective. The thing is, 90 per cent of Australian students surveyed (in Years 2 to 3) say they want to help others.[3]

Volunteering is good for both the mind and the body, because it builds community and diminishes loneliness by reducing stress and social isolation and, by developing a solid support system. It enhances social skills, builds mental strength, and increases self-confidence and life satisfaction. It has even been shown to lessen symptoms of chronic pain or heart disease. But more importantly, volunteering teaches us that everyone is valuable, thus developing ethical behaviour.[4]

Even toddlers and preschoolers learn about community responsibility, compassion, empathy and tolerance through volunteering. Children who volunteer are more likely to grow up to be adults with these skills. You can start by asking children how they might like to help others.[5]

Family volunteering ideas:
- Put together books, toys, board games and activity boxes for children at a local hospital.
- Donate to a food pantry – children can help choose items.
- Create Christmas boxes for charities.
- Walk or run to raise funds to fight disease.
- Take muffins to the staff on duty at nursing homes, fire or police stations on public holidays.
- Clean up your local park, neighbourhood or beach (supervise your children closely).
- Deliver meals to an elderly neighbour or someone who is ill.
- Be kind to animals. If you can't have a pet, volunteer to do weekend or respite care at local shelters.
- Support and become involved with advocacy groups. This will make it apparent to your children what your values are as a family. This also gives you a reason to talk about the topic. Our family supports Collective Shout, who speak out against sexualised images and

advertising in Australia. We also financially support children through Compassion. I am an ambassador for International Justice Mission Australia, who fight against the cybersex trafficking of children in Australia and our neighbouring countries.

Overall, when we volunteer we notice a subtle shift in ourselves, because our work makes a difference to others. As human beings, when we work for something greater than ourselves we develop moral character. When giving and volunteering become family habits we teach children about the value of others, especially those who are vulnerable.

Key Messages

- Teaching gratitude and responsibility is an inoculation against entitlement – parents who teach appreciation of others and that life is about more than ourselves and what we want in the moment set their children up to be kind and empathetic adults.
- Encourage your child to volunteer and help in the community, because when we teach children to look outwards, their own needs and problems come into perspective.

Empathy: 'Spread kindness like confetti.'

When the whole world is silent, even one voice becomes powerful.

– Malala Yousafzai

I believe that empathy is the most important skill for teaching young people how to have healthy relationships. In the West we have come to pursue happiness through personal power, consumption and accumulation. We pay too little attention to teaching kindness or looking outwards in relation to happiness.

This is evident in the findings by Harvard University's Making Caring Common Project.[1] On interviewing thousands of middle and high-school students, researchers surmised that when asked to rank their top priorities, around 80 per cent of the young people surveyed value personal achievement and personal happiness over caring for others (only valued by 20 per cent of students). Additionally, when ranking specific values students consistently rated hard work and self-interest over fairness. Not that hard work is a bad quality in itself;

rather, when caring and fairness are not prioritised, a lower bar is set for many ethical qualities, which leads to all kinds of harmful behaviour, including cruelty, disrespect, dishonesty and cheating.

What also became apparent through the survey is that although we *say* we value caring and kindness in our children, most young people believe their parents value academic achievement more. This is what the researchers call the rhetoric–reality gap. Basically, parents are not walking the talk – we are not demonstrating practically what we say (and even believe) about kindness.[2]

The good news is that empathy – trying to undertand or imagine yourself in another person's place, rather than from your own point of view – is something that can be taught at each stage of children's development. As we teach our children about relationships, it is helpful to view empathy and learning to respond to others with dignity and kindness as skills that need practice. Just like in sport, where we need to continually work at our physical fitness in order to get better on the field, we need to exercise our empathy muscles, so that we maintain strength in this area of relationships. By modelling empathetic behaviour and pointing out situations that call for empathy, we begin to induce feelings for other people.

Essentially, empathy is seeing and responding to another's humanity, and sexualised culture obliterates empathy because it treats human beings as objects.[3] Research indicates that viewing sexualised images (of both men and women) leads to the belief that the objectified targets possess 'less mind and moral status', which is basically a denial of thoughts and emotions. When one person objectifies another (discussed in detail in Conversation #9) it is difficult – nay, impossible – to treat that person with empathy.

TRY THIS:

There are three types of empathy, listed by the world's leading expert on Emotional Intelligence, Daniel Goleman,[4] which I believe we can help children become fluent in. Try discussing each with your child.

Cognitive empathy – the ability to identify how the other person feels and consider what they might be thinking.

- 'Did you notice anyone looking sad today? What do you think was going on for them?'
- 'Who did you make eye contact with this week, while they were talking?' Eye contact demonstrates listening.
- 'Have you noticed anyone who might need to know someone cares about them? What did you notice?'

Emotional empathy – the ability to physically feel what other people feel, almost as though their emotions were contagious.

- 'What is one kind thing somebody else did for you today?'
- 'Has someone treated you unkindly? How did that make you feel? How could you treat others so that they never have to feel the same way because of you?'
- 'Did you notice an animal or a person in pain? How do you think they felt?'
- Use stories from books or television as opportunities for kids to practise perspective-taking skills. Ask questions such as, 'What do the characters think, believe, want, or feel? How do we know?'

Practical empathy (which Goleman calls Empathic Concern) – it is important to model not only grasping a person's problem and feeling along with them, but also being spontaneously moved to help where you can. This can be done in the everyday interactions our children have with those around them, and also through the volunteering activities discussed in Conversation #14.

- 'What is one kind thing you did today?'
- 'Who do you think might need a smile from you today?'
- 'How could you show a person that you care about them?'
- 'How might we show your grandparents (or local grandfriends) that we love and honour them this week?'

Remember my friend's family value from Chapter 3 – kindness? *'In the future, people won't remember anything about you, other than how they* felt *when they were around you. Remember to be kind.'* Real meaning and true happiness come from thinking about other people – and from actions that bring meaning or joy to other people's lives.

Key Messages
- Empathy and treating people with dignity and kindness is something that can be taught at each stage of a child's development. As we teach our children about relationships, it is helpful to view empathy and kindness as skills that need practice.
- Real meaning and true happiness come from thinking about other people – and from actions that bring meaning or joy to other people's lives.

SECTION 3

My Conversation with Schools

'What is the role of schools in raising ethical students?'

Parents and schools need to play an active role in monitoring and boundary setting for young people in relation to cyber safety, but this must be done within the context of trusting and respectful relationships.

– The Australian Psychological Society,[1] 2016

If you work in a school you are here, like me, because you recognise the elephant in the classroom. You know it lurks there, follows kids home and sits on their beds at night while their parents sleep – blissfully unaware. The elephant I am referring to is, of course, porn. Yet I find that schools are still somewhat jumpy about addressing inappropriate online content and porn culture directly. Perhaps some are afraid of offending the chairman of the board, or believe that they won't tackle it well in their lessons, or think that students don't want to hear from teachers? I don't know, but young people's exposure to pornography is everybody's concern, everybody's duty of care, and the collective turning of a blind eye to this problem equates to the cultural grooming of children.

As much as I believe the role of sex education and values education to be primarily a parent's responsibility, the reality is that many parents, through cultural, religious and personal reasons, either can't, won't or don't know how to talk about it. If schools avoid covering tough topics, the danger is that many children are left with a gaping void when they are faced with big issues, like online porn. Our young people need the adults in their lives to help them understand that porn is not a healthy reality. Schools need to step in and support families. Schools need to provide tools for both parents and the students in their care.

With most sex education either focused narrowly on abstinence, or on how not to get pregnant or contract sexually transmitted diseases, the majority of students believe their school sex education to be grossly inadequate. The encouraging news is that 65 per cent of 18- to 25-year-old survey respondents said they 'wished that they had received guidance on some emotional aspect of romantic relationships in a health or sex education class at school'.[2] Students want to engage, in depth, with teachers about aspects like love and how to develop a mature, healthy relationship.

A word of warning

We've seen schools hauled before a Royal Commission because of their fear or reluctance to get involved in reports of sexual misconduct and abuse in the past. This may seem harsh, but I believe it needs to be said: I fear that schools' current reluctance to talk openly about the proliferation of pornography use, by students within school grounds, will be the Royal Commission for a new generation of trauma victims, if the schools continue to do nothing.

A note to boarding schools

In my opinion, schools form the village where children grow up, even more so if children attend boarding schools. I am gravely concerned that many boarding schools are failing this generation of children due to a lack of boundaries around technology. Just as parents have had to adapt their parenting styles around technology in their homes, so should boarding houses, because many parents place their children into the care of schools as surrogate parents, for entire weeks or months (or years) at a time.

Tradition is a fabulous thing, but some traditions are dangerous and we know they can lead to lifelong pain. Just because something has been done a certain way for 100 years doesn't make it healthy. Things have changed. Schools, we absolutely must address this! Our duty of care dictates that we talk about the content our children access, and do our utmost to mitigate the effects within our walls. We need serious and urgent conversations about the safety of our students in these settings.

This letter was given to me by a teacher and boarding house master after his concerns were not heeded by the school where he worked:

I have been a teacher for over 20 years and have worked in boarding at two different schools for more than 7 of those years. During my time working at my most recent school, I was shocked at the spread and ease of access that boys had to pornography and other inappropriate material.

The boarding house had a vertical age structure, with ages ranging from 13 to 18 years old. All students were boys, with about 50 in the house. There was a housemaster and 2 other adult staff who took turns in supervising the boys in the house. So the staff-to-student ratio was quite high, with one staff member looking after more than 50 boys when on duty.

Most students in the boarding house had their own (parent-supplied) laptop. Students were able to connect their laptops to the school's computer network. The school network had filters on it designed to prevent boys from accessing what the school deemed were inappropriate sites, but in my experience these were easily bypassed by the boys in a couple of ways:

1. *By using web proxy servers designed to get around filtering and blocking by institutions such as schools, or*
2. *By the boys purchasing their own plug-in 4G modems to give them open access to the internet, completely bypassing the school network altogether. A number of boys would also tether their smartphones to their laptops to achieve the same purpose.*

So the school's filtered network, which was supposed to give parents some peace of mind about what their sons were getting up to on the net, was in fact not doing much at all to prevent access. Downloaded pornography was readily available and shared around the house using portable hard-drive players. Students would swap hard drives to share what they had downloaded. There was some sharing between older students and younger boys. These hard drives would be confiscated when found but their small size meant that they were easily hidden in a student's belongings.

At lights out, all students would be in their beds. It was not uncommon to see them making a little 'nest' in their bed by pulling their sheets over their heads so they could watch their laptops in bed after lights out and the staff member had gone home for the evening.

The housemaster in charge of the house very much turned a blind eye to what was going on in his house. I did not feel supported at all in trying to change the culture or behaviour going on in the house. Other houses had staff in charge with a different attitude to the problems outlined above and I understand there was not the same level of sharing of inappropriate material going on.

Another area of concern was boys playing violent video games on their laptops and public computers in the house. Again this was tolerated and allowed by the housemaster. I can especially remember a Year 8 boy showing me a section of a game (I think it was Grand Theft Auto*) unlocked by a 'cheat' code that enabled graphic sexual acts to be simulated as part of the game. So the boys were very open to sharing with each other and even staff about what they could do in the game. The behaviour had become normalised in the house and part of the culture, making it very hard if not impossible to change from my point of view as a junior member of staff in the house.*

Frustrated after 3 years working in the house, trying to confront inappropriate behaviour whenever I came across it and feeling no support from the senior housemaster, I decided that it was time to change jobs and I left the school.

(Name withheld to protect the teacher's privacy)

How do we implement these discussions in schools?

It is not as difficult to implement appropriate discussions in schools as you might imagine. In fact, there are things you are doing already that form a solid foundation for talking about porn culture, respect and loving relationships. If your head teacher says you don't have space in your very full curriculum, tell them you do.

Wellbeing in schools

Schools need to focus on kids being strong – not only on what is going wrong. Young people need guidance and opportunities to explore what a strong character looks like and ideas for how to live well. We absolutely must incorporate wellbeing programs into our school curriculum. Our kids' lives depend on it.

Teaching empathy in the playground

Rather than focusing on the '3Rs' of old, schools nowadays are so much better at teaching the whole child. Schools recognise their role as mentors, and even surrogate parents, for the children who don't have supportive carers to put in place some of the ideas held in this book. In fact, many schools understand the importance of developing a social emotional curriculum, because students who feel threatened and are distracted by a hostile culture find learning more difficult – whereas developing a child's empathy, the ability to consider another's perspective, and manage their own emotions and actions, leads to a significantly positive impact on academic performance, graduation rates and economic outcomes for students. More importantly, we now know that long-term fulfilment and mental wellbeing do not ultimately come from academic achievement, job status or financial gain. Rather, flourishing human beings are those who enjoy meaningful human connection, demonstrate a sense of responsibility, and purposefully contribute to something outside of themselves.

Hence, it matters that schools teach young people how to be kind, because a caring outlook is linked to positive life outcomes. The great news is that the research shows that social and emotional skills, including empathy, kindness and compassion, can be taught and learned.

Classroom and whole-school project ideas for teaching empathy

- **Within current subjects**
  Start by encouraging critical thinking about empathy, using movies and books within school subjects like history, English, and personal development, health and physical education.

- **An ethics-based school culture**

Practically teach students to become ethical human beings by establishing something like a Social Justice Warriors group, Everyday Hero projects or a Compassion Club.

- **Using journals**

Incorporate a short period of time for students to create a written or image-based weekly journal, where they record acts of kindness toward people in their lives. (So as not to overload a teacher's week, perhaps this could be done in place of writing about their own weekend activities or holidays at times?) Students only need 5 minutes a week to record these and to plan something for the following week. This isn't about teaching writing skills (although writing skills are likely to improve in the process), it is about developing a habit of mindful empathy, i.e. practising empathy until it becomes an inbuilt character trait. I do not believe that empathy projects should be rewarded with medals or marks; rather, they should only be seen by parents and the class teacher. Empathy should be part of doing the right thing, not about getting noticed for doing the right thing.

- **Volunteering**

Whole class or year group volunteering might take place during the last week of every term. These days can be part of the school excursion plan and could include local park or beach clean-ups, reading stories to and playing with children at local preschools, chatting with the locals or doing gardening at a retirement village, or collecting and delivering goods for women's shelters and children's hospitals.

Resilient Youth Australia runs Students Create the Future workshops, which are held at schools during school hours. These workshops activate resilience through student-led change projects.

- **Thank-you week**

How about implementing a thank-you week into the school year? (My children's school does this really well.) Classes write letters to a special person who has made a difference in their lives. Year groups invite local police officers, MPs or community workers to a lunch or tea hosted by students. Alternatively, students visit hospitals or fire stations with thank-you cards and notes. Students lead this initiative and can be as creative as they like, with staff supervision.

- **Digital citizenship**

I would say that all schools now incorporate digital citizenship programs. Many provide opportunities for learning responsible online citizenship through programs like the eSmart Digital Licence, done through the Alannah and Madeline Foundation.

Additionally, rather than just teaching the online 'don'ts', teachers need to be sharing stories about what works well. For example, I met 14-year-old Sally after a seminar I ran at her school. Sally told me about a tricky group of girls she hung out with at school. She recalled a time when she had been on the receiving end of social exclusion on Instagram. A group of girlfriends had 'secretly' planned a dinner excursion to a nice restaurant in the city, and the event was broadcast once in full swing, with girls posting and tagging pictures of their 'amazing night'. Sally recalled her pain and confusion, as these were girls she sat with at lunch and she had not been included. She said she had cried that evening and questioned many things about herself. However, some weeks later Sally attended a party at someone's house. When she arrived at the party, Sally realised that there was a girl excluded from the party because she and her friend had had an argument. When Sally got home, she said she privately messaged this girl to tell her she had missed seeing her that night and was sorry to see she was not there. The excluded girl was amazed by Sally's message. She responded with something like, 'Thank you so much! I thought no one noticed that I wasn't there.' I asked Sally what had made her decide to reach out to this girl. Sally said, 'I knew what it felt like to be in her place. It's what I wished someone had done for me. So I just did it.' Sally's story of empathy and private messaging a victim is in fact exactly what research has told us is helpful to those who are on the receiving end of online bullying or exclusion.

Colin Wood, the head of a middle school in Sydney that I have worked with for many years, devised the ROCKonline idea to help children navigate the online spaces. I love it, because it incorporates teaching children they are both love-WORTHY and can be love-ABLE when making decisions with screens.

	Does this ROCK for others?	Does this ROCK for me?
Respect	Does this respect others? Is it telling the truth? Does it need to be said?	Does this respect me? Is it the truth? Can I make my own choices?
Obedience	Am I obeying the rules set for me by my parents, the law and the school?	Does this obey online rules from parents, the law and the school?
Courtesy	How can I be courteous? Have I said this in the best way?	Is courtesy being shown to me? Does it need to be said? Are they thinking about me?
Kindness	Am I kind online? How do I make the effort to love others?	Is it kind? Are you part of a conversation that shares love?
	Read again before you send and make the choice to ROCK.	If it doesn't ROCK tell your parents.

It provides teachers with opportunities to talk about what kids, like Sally, are doing well online (i.e. demonstrating that they are love-ABLE). I like how point 'O' (Obedience), about adhering to boundaries, is only one part of four of the discussions about online behaviour. The majority of the model teaches children to think about their values. It helps them to consider whether there is mutual Respect, Courtesy and Kindness on their devices. It is such a positive tool, which uses questions to encourage critical thinking and personal ownership of choices, rather than being a list of online 'don'ts'.

Body safety and personal boundaries lessons

From preschools through to high schools, body safety and personal boundaries should be taught at least once a year. This could be done using picture books, holding student seminars or discussing current news or movies, and should include parent training.

Object to objectification through critical media analysis

There is nothing empathetic about treating someone as an object. This is something that can be taught and unpacked quite early on in the school years. Primary teachers might use cartoons like *Tom and Jerry*, in a fun way, to look for times when one of the characters is a stand-in for an object. For example, when Jerry repeatedly hits Tom on the head with a mallet, he stands in for a nail. For teens, teachers can use examples from a current television series the students are watching, or celebrity feeds they follow on social media. Students might sit in groups with questions to spark critical thinking about objectification and media messages.

Question starters:
- 'What is that picture trying to make you think/feel?'
- 'Is that toy ad trying to change your mind about something?'

- 'What do you think that music video says about the role of women or minority groups?'
- 'How does that movie leave out truths about real-life friendships?'
- 'What might be a better way to treat that character?'
- 'What do you think that person might be feeling after that incident? How would you feel if that were you?'

Respect and relationships

Sex education isn't the only place in schools where young people can gain insights into respectful relationships, romance and sexuality. English, history, music and social science courses are some of the subjects full of opportunities to talk about relationships and love. Given how frequently children are exposed to sports stars who are bad role models, sports coaches can play a key role in talking about romance, sex and respectful behaviour. Sexually degrading and homophobic talk on buses and in locker rooms can be challenged by respected school teachers. Sport can be a fantastic vehicle for cultivating a climate of equality and respect for women.

What 13- and 14-year-old students want to know about relationships:

As a guide for schools and parents wanting to know what students are curious about, the following are unedited questions that 13- and 14-year-old male and female students ask me anonymously at the end of my Respectful Relationships seminars every year. These are the questions students say they wish a parent or adult would answer for them. These are the questions they ask Google, if there is no adult to talk to:

How do you make the smart choice when the decisions are difficult?
What is a reasonable age to have a boyfriend?

What age do you recommend is a good age to have a romantic relationship?

How do you know if you really like someone?

Why are the boys mean to the girls?

I like a boy but he always goes on about how he only likes girls with big boobs and a big butt. What do I do?

Why are girls put down more than guys?

How do you know if a guy likes you?

What is a good conversation starter if I have never talked to a guy?

How should men view women?

What do you do if you are in a toxic relationship but you can't get out of it?

What even is love?

Is it okay to be scared of losing someone?

How do you know if you are in love with someone?

Why can't boys be nice to girls when they are on their period?

I believe everyone is struggling. How do you support others if they ask for help?

What do girls usually think of guys as a whole?

How can you gain trust in an adult?

What do guys expect of girls at our age?

A boy keeps asking me for nudes but even when I say no he pressures until I do … what should I do?

What 13- and 14-year-old students want to know about their bodies and sex:

When someone says yes once, does it mean that it means yes always?

What does it mean if your boobs hurt?

How is sex a good thing?

Do you have to wait until you are married to have sex?

Is it alright to masturbate?

Is masturbation normal today?

How long does one sexual intercourse take?

What is actually safe sex? What should you do?

What do you think about birth control pills?

Can you have sex when you are pregnant?

How do people have sex when they don't learn how to?

Does sex hurt?

Why do people want to post a video of themselves having sex on the internet?

What is oral sex?

What is the average age of girls when they lose their virginity in Australia?

How does a sperm find its way into an egg?

Why does it hurt when you get hit in the private parts?

How do you know if the sperm is in?

How can you tell if your wife is ready for sex?

Who wears condoms (males or females)?

Why does it hurt when you have sex?

How can you tell if you have a sexual disease?

What is an orgasm?

When people have sex do both men and women orgasm or is it just one of them?

Is anal sex bad?

I feel bad for not having big boobs. What do I do?

Pornography as poison

It is vital that schools have a plan for talking about pornography with students. Be preventative and empower both parents and students by raising awareness regularly, like you would with alcohol or drug issues. Schools can suggest books for parents, run student seminars, hold parent information evenings and list online resources in newsletters. Model it as normal to talk about. Also, be restorative for when pornography use is reported or accessed by students of different ages. By all means put appropriate boundaries in place, but don't shame the student/s involved. Students' personal shame will be magnified already when their pornography use is exposed by adults. Provide the parents and students with access to support and help.

There are things schools are doing already where this can easily be incorporated. Discussions about pornography fit easily into programs on a healthy digital diet or digital citizenship, alcohol and binge drinking, family violence and bullying. In fact, they must be part of these lessons.

- **Alcohol**

Talk with young people about the mix of binge drinking with a default porn culture mentality and how it leads to a toxic recipe for disaster.

- **Unhealthy digital diets**

When schools chat about social media, online privacy and great apps, porn can be highlighted as the poison of technology. More and more schools have started a 'no phones to be seen during school hours' policy. Technology is still used under supervision in the classroom, but students are encouraged to engage, talk and be active during recess and lunch – because we know how vital movement is for getting the very best we can out of brains in the classroom. This also helps schools minimise the potential for sharing of inappropriate, even illegal, images while on school property.

This is not impossible for schools to implement. One family I know met with their son's principal at an all-boys school, because their 13-year-old came home with reports of boys sharing pornographic files during school times, even during class. The principal dismissed the parents' concerns as their being unwelcoming of new technology and teaching styles, and even suggested that it might just be their own son's 'problem' – until the school was suddenly dealing with the police on a matter a few months later. To the school's credit, a year down the track they began a new policy of 'no phones to be seen during school hours'. Students were encouraged to use the school office phone to contact parents if there was an emergency (which is good for all sorts of OH&S reasons – when a student is hurt or sick it is the school's responsibility to know about it and care for the student until a parent is notified). Another school has a class captain or student leader collect phones in a sealed container at the start of the day. The containers are taken and stored on a shelf in the school office and the same student collects the box before the end of the day and hands the phones back to their classmates. A different school requires students to ensure their phones are completely out of sight during school hours, unless needed for a classroom task. Schools are figuring out systems that work for them and have seen great gains in student engagement and interaction overall.

- **Anti-bullying programs**

If schools talk about and spend money on white ribbons and anti-bullying programs but don't get to the root of these issues, they are speaking into the wind, because pornography is bullying and sexual violence 101. Schools need to address sexual bullying and revenge porn as forms of bullying, harassment and violence. They need to employ a zero-tolerance policy for porn sharing or rape 'jokes' at school or at school events. Students need to hear the message that porn culture is not a part of your school culture.

- **Address pornography directly**

The Childline survey in the UK indicates that more than two-thirds of 11- to 18-year-olds believe porn should be discussed as part of sex education.[3]

This is what 13- and 14-year-old students want to know about sex and pornography. This is what I get asked at every seminar I run on pornography:

How do I stop watching porn/masturbating?

Why is it so hard to get off of it [porn]?

How do you stop yourself from being exposed to pornographic photos? E.g. If you are on a website and a photo for an ad pops up?

My friend is addicted to porn and masturbation and such. How do I help him?

How do you overcome the addiction of porn?

How do you stop porn?

Is there a way to forget the visions of forced viewing of porn by someone else?

How do you stop sexual ads coming up on websites?

Is it true in Kings Cross that you can watch sex on stage?

Do sex scenes in movies count as pornography even if they don't show any genitalia?

Why did I want to watch porn at a young age? Is it bad that I watched porn at a young age?

What's the best way to block porn if you haven't been exposed yet?

I've been watching porn for 4 years and my parents don't know. How do I get help?

What are some ways to stop porn addiction?

On the internet I have seen articles of people having intercourse with animals – what are your thoughts on that?

Is it bad to watch porn?

How is porn bad for people?

What's the difference between sex and porn?

What if you are forced to watch porn and can't get out of it?

Why is porn addictive?

How do you stop yourself from seeing pornography once it's an addiction?

Why do people get addicted to porn?

Teens need to hear from lots of people, not only their parents, about porn as a poisonous script for sex. They need to hear that a lot of the myths and stereotypes we are trying to combat in school bullying and self-worth programs are reinforced through porn – porn reinforces gender stereotypes, racism, body image issues and even distorted thinking about penis size. This topic ought to be covered at least once a year. Yes, it is difficult, but schools can get expert speakers to kickstart the conversation and to train teachers how to do this, until they feel comfortable running programs on their own.

Give young people opportunities to own their choices

A few years ago I spoke to students at Georges River Grammar in Sydney as part of their media literacy program. After my session, the male staff and students decided to develop a commitment pledge to respect the women and girls in their school and wider community. The students came up with the wording themselves and then each boy signed his own pledge in front of his peers. This was powerful, because it came from and was developed by the students.

Respect for Women

I _____ will do my best to show respect and consideration for women every day by committing to the following:
[list ways of showing respect and consideration]
This commitment is made in front of my peers and I promise to do all that I can to uphold each of my promises.

Signed_____Date_____

Rites-of-passage programs

I believe that the modern world is poorer for leaving behind some of the richness that came with rites of passage. Healthy rites-of-passage periods taught young people the skills they needed and placed on them the appropriate expectations for taking their place as the new adults in society. When done well by loving mentors, rites of passage helped to intentionally and deliberately guide young people into adulthood. Unfortunately, many young people these days are left to fill this child-to-adult chasm by looking to celebrity and sport culture, or by inventing their own meaning for what it is to grow up, which is often found in alcohol and sexualised and dangerous behaviours.

My dear friend Andrew Lines is an educator who has developed a program called The Rite Journey, which is now implemented in schools all around the world.[4] It is designed to support the development of self-aware, responsible and resilient adults. It reinvents the traditional process of a rite of passage to assist in transforming the adolescent from dependency to responsibility. The Rite Journey is part of the students' lives for an entire year, which encourages ongoing development of self-awareness and builds strong, honest and respectful relationships with peers, parents and teachers. The boys' program is designed to specifically help boys to see and learn how important it is to share how they are feeling, to seek help when it is needed, to tell their story and to care for their hearts. What I love about The Rite Journey is that it can be moulded and adapted to a school's culture and ethos, and it purposely engages adults by welcoming and guiding them into the lives of their teens at various parts of the journey.

Programs like The Rite Journey form a wonderful scaffold for schools to implement discussions and activities for raising empathic, ethical and respectful young people.

Key Messages

- Students want to engage, in depth, with teachers about aspects like love and how to develop a mature, healthy relationship.
- Developing a child's empathy, the ability to consider another's perspective, and manage their own emotions and actions, leads to a significantly positive impact on academic performance, graduation rates and economic outcomes for students.
- Schools need to be preventative when it comes to pornography, and empower both parents and students by raising awareness regularly, like they would with alcohol or drug issues. Schools can suggest books for parents, run student seminars, hold parent information evenings and list online resources in newsletters. Model it as normal to talk about. Schools must also be restorative for when pornography use is reported or accessed by students of different ages.
- Many young people these days are left to fill the child-to-adult chasm by looking to celebrity and sport culture, or by inventing their own meaning for what it is to grow up, which is often found in alcohol and sexualised and dangerous behaviours. But healthy rites-of-passage periods can teach young people the skills they need and place on them the appropriate expectations for taking their place as the new adults in society.

They *will* be okay

Every parent wishes for their child to develop meaningful relationships in their lifetime, because we know it is through relationships that we find true happiness. Our own relationships with our children lay the foundation for them understanding 'how to do relationships well'. We demonstrate what it looks like to both give and receive. It is through these relationships that they learn that they are worthy of love, and that being consistently hurt or even abused is never okay. It is where they learn about times of selflessness – that others' needs and feelings matter too. It is through learning how to respond to the good times, the tough times and the everything-in-between times that our children develop relational resilience.

Sometimes we might feel as though this responsibility on us as parents is overwhelming. We worry about whether we are 'getting it right'. But the wonderful news is that strong relationships don't happen in one night or with one talk. Relationships happen through the many and unique conversations, traditions and interactions within each family. All of the ups and downs build trust.

Each of the conversations in this book will not (in fact – they should not) happen in one sitting, one day or even one year. And it is never too late to start a conversation if you have not had one with your teen yet – because they still need you. So if at times a discussion seems daunting, hold on to the fact that the conversations will flow a little easier the more you have them. Your children learn that nothing is taboo, because you aren't afraid to address the awkward topics. As you deliberately parent in this way, the conversations will slowly unfold at the times your child needs them. And the end result? A resilient and empathetic adult, who understands their uniqueness and who positively contributes to making our world a better place.

ACKNOWLEDGEMENTS

In Chapter 2 I talk about the village. Everything we do in life comes out of being part of 'a tribe'. This is thanks to those in mine. Both my professional and personal journeys are made up of many connections that shaped me into who I am.

Thank you to the people who taught me and inspired me to go into teaching and to work with young people in the first place. My Grade 1 teacher Mrs Tessa York (who was my very first favourite teacher), my high-school English teacher Miss Brown, and my Zulu teacher Alyson Kieswetter – I loved school because of you. You each made teaching and working with young people look like a wonderful way to spend your day.

There are those in the very early years of my career, as both a teacher and a psychologist, who helped me develop my ideas and practices. Thank you to the very first mentor teachers in my life, Yvonne Souris and Barbara Vincent. Dr Herbie Staples, the principal at a school I worked at who graciously sat with a feisty young South African teacher as I wrestled with developing my teaching style – you still continue to encourage me today. People like Barbara Pawlowicz, who helped me through my post-grad studies (while I was heavily pregnant) and grew alongside me in our love for psychology. Dr Rebecca Loundar who walked me through the whole psychology registration process and taught me a great deal about our profession.

Thank you to Dr Tina Lamont for encouraging me in one of my first jobs as a school counsellor in Australia. Dr Edwin Boyce, for your kindness and support, from my early years in Australian Education right through to the present. My friend and colleague Colin Wood, for your vision and for allowing me to try out new seminar topics, before speaking on the harms of pornography was even something that schools would consider. My teaching and counselling colleagues, who demonstrate daily, the impact that mentors can truly have on young people.

To Andrew Fuller, who I have admired professionally for many years, I am so excited to have you write the foreword for my book. Thank you to the many people who contributed sections, agreed to be quoted and shared personal stories with me for this book. It is so much richer because of these.

Thank you so much to my publisher, Sophie Hamley, for believing in this book and taking me on an amazing journey. My editors Brigid Mullane and Kylie Mason for challenging my writing and making me look fantastic. Sarah Brooks, Emily Arbis, Alana Kelly, Tania Mackenzie-Cooke and the rest of the team at Hachette, for all the behind the scenes stuff that no one realises make a book happen. I am so very grateful to you all.

My parents Brian and Desire Easton, thank you for your consistent love and support throughout my life. My in-laws Mike and Maureen Smart – for raising the type of good man I write about in this book. Thank you for your legacy. All four of you are incredible grandparents to our children. My brother Paul (my first friend), Sue, Mark and Ros – family is everything! The older I grow the more I know this to be true.

My best friend, Loraine – I am so glad we both moved to Australia and that we met! Thank you for the long weekly coffees where we always run out of time, your encouragement for me to keep writing and for helping me sift through my thoughts for this book.

Greg, my husband, closest friend and my daily example of what a good man looks like. You are always so full of energy and have an incredible passion for life. You are one of the deepest thinkers I know and you have been my biggest supporter. You have challenged me, helped sharpen my thinking and encouraged me to keep going when it has been hard. I love you with my whole heart. My beautiful children, Jayson, Daena and Liam – the reason I write this book. Thank you for your patience (and cups of tea) on those long evenings of writing and editing. I am so proud of each of you and I love being your mum. I love you my family! And finally, my God, who teaches me daily how to promote justice, to love kindness and to walk humbly. I am always learning.

ENDNOTES

Chapter 1 – Helping kids flourish

1   Russ Pratt, 'The "porn genie" is out of the bottle: Understanding and responding to the impact of pornography on young people', *InPsych,* Vol 37 Issue 2, 2015, www.psychology.org.au/inpsych/2015/april/pratt

2   South Eastern Centre Against Sexual Assault (SECASA), 'Harm being done to Australian children through access to pornography on the Internet', Submission 334, www.aph.gov.au/DocumentStore.ashx?id=424b21a8-e82b-483e-a69d-a11fee613a59&subId=410352

Chapter 2 – Strong relationships are where healthy relationships thrive

1   Harvard Second Generation Study, www.adultdevelopmentstudy.org

2   Mission Australia, Youth survey report, 2016, www.missionaustralia.com.au/documents/research/young-people-research/677-mission-australia-youth-survey-report-2016

3   Patricia M Greenfield, 'Inadvertent exposure to pornography on the Internet: Implications of peer-to-peer file-sharing networks for child development and families', *Journal of Applied Developmental Psychology*, Vol 25 Issue 6, 2004, www.sciencedirect.com/science/article/pii/S0193397304000814

4   Making Caring Common Project, 'The talk: How adults can promote young people's healthy relationships and prevent misogyny and sexual harassment', Harvard University, https://mcc.gse.harvard.edu/thetalk

5   Kathleen Denny, Melissa Milkie and Kei Nomaguchi, 'Does the amount of time mothers spend with children or adolescents matter?', *Journal of Marriage and Family*, Vol 77 Issue 2, 2015, onlinelibrary.wiley.com/doi/abs/10.1111/jomf.12170

6   Giulia Dotti Sani and Judith Treas, 'Educational gradients in parents' child-care time across countries, 1965–2012', *Journal of Marriage and Family*, Vol 78 Issue 4, 2016, onlinelibrary.wiley.com/doi/abs/10.1111/jomf.12305

7   Joseph Allen, Joanna Chango, Elenda Hessel, Emily Loeb, Megan Schad and Joseph Tan, 'Long-term predictions from early adolescent attachment state of mind to romantic relationship behaviors', *Research on Adolescence*, Vol 26 Issue 4, 2016, onlinelibrary.wiley.com/doi/10.1111/jora.12256/full

8   Gretchen Livingston and Kim Parker, '7 facts about American dads', Pew Research Centre, 2018, pewrsr.ch/2sf9Bqi

9   Leanne Lester and Stacey Waters, 'A review of Australian evidence of the impact of fathering', *The Fathering Project*, University of Western Australia, 2015, thefatheringproject.org/fpwp/wp-content/uploads/2015/10/Fathering-Data-Analysis-Report-SUMMARY-EXCL-COMMENTS.pdf

10   Sarah Allen and Kerry Daly, 'The effects of father involvement: A summary of the research evidence', *The FII-ONews*, Vol 1, 2002, www.ecdip.org/docs/pdf/IF%20 Father%20Res%20Summary%20(KD).pdf

11   Estée Lambin and Lisa Wood, 'How fathers and father figures can shape child health and wellbeing', *The Fathering Project*, University of Western Australia, thefatheringproject.org/fpwp/wp-content/uploads/2015/11/New-Fathering-Research.pdf

12   Sarah Flood, Ann Meier and Kelly Musick, 'How parents fare: Mothers' and fathers' subjective well-being in time with children', *American Sociological Review*, Vol 81 Issue 5, 2016, journals.sagepub.com/doi/abs/10.1177/0003122416663917

13   Linda Nielsen, 'Young adult daughters' relationships with their fathers: Review of recent research', *Marriage & Family Review*, 2014, www.orgscience.com/uploads/library/74caae3d4e2232c5d411d6c7703e736d.pdf

14   Jennifer Katz and Erika van der Kloet, 'The first man in her life: Father emotional responsiveness during adolescence and college women's sexual refusal behaviors', *The American Journal of Family Therapy*, 2010, www.tandfonline.com/doi/abs/10.1 080/01926187.2010.493474

15   Ondrej Kalina et al, 'Mother's and father's monitoring is more important than parental social support regarding sexual risk behaviour among 15-year-old adolescents', *The European Journal of Contraception and Reproductive Health Care*, 2013, www.tandfonline.com/doi/abs/10.3109/13625187.2012.752450

16   Analisa Arroyo, Ashley Randall and Paul Wright, 'Father-daughter communication about sex moderates the association between exposure to MTV's *16 and Pregnant/Teen Mom* and female students' pregnancy-risk behavior', *Sexuality and Culture*, Vol 17 Issue 1, 2013, asu.pure.elsevier.com/en/publications/father-daughter-communication-about-sex-moderates-the-association

17   Bruce Ellis et al, 'Does Father Absence Place Daughters at Special Risk for Early Sexual Activity and Teenage Pregnancy?', *Child Development*, Vol 74 Issue 3, 2003, www.ncbi.nlm.nih.gov/pmc/articles/PMC2764264/

18   Leah East, Debra Jackson and Louise O'Brien, 'Father absence and adolescent development: A review of the literature', *Journal of Child Healthcare*, Vol 10 Issue 4, 2006, www.ncbi.nlm.nih.gov/pubmed/17101621

19   Joan Luby et al, 'Preschool is a sensitive period for the influence of maternal support on the trajectory of hippocampal development', *PNAS*, 2016, www.pnas.org/content/113/20/5742.abstract

20   Joan Luby et al, 2016

Chapter 3 – 7 tips for a firm foundation to build conversations upon

1   Tim Kasser, Richard Koestner and Natahsa Lekes, 'Early family experiences and adult values: A 26-year, prospective longitudinal study', *Personality and Social Psychology Bulletin*, 2002, journals.sagepub.com/doi/abs/10.1177/0146167202289011

Chapter 4 – Age-appropriate conversations

1   Michael Yogman et al, 'The power of play: A pediatric role in enhancing development in young children', *American Academy of Pediatrics Clinical Report*, 2018, pediatrics.aappublications.org/content/early/2018/08/16/peds.2018-2058

Relationship Intelligence

1   Daniel Goleman, *Emotional Intelligence*, Random House, 2005

Conversation #1 – Body Safety

1 Educate2Empower, 'About Jayneen Sanders', e2epublishing.info/jay
2 Royal Commission into Institutional Responses to Child Sexual Abuse, 'Identifying and disclosing sexual abuse', 2017, www.childabuseroyalcommission. gov.au/sites/default/files/final_report_-_volume_4_identifying_and_disclosing_ child_sexual_abuse.pdf
3 Imperial Chemical Industries, 'The ICI report on the secrets of the senses', blindnessandarts.com/papers/ICIsensessynopsisdocument.pdf

Conversation #2 – Emotional Intelligence

1 Saz Ahmed, Amanda Bittencourt-Hewitt and Catherine Sebastian, 'Neurocognitive bases of emotion regulation development in adolescence', *Developmental Cognitive Neuroscience*, Vol 15, 2015, www.sciencedirect.com/ science/article/pii/S1878929315000717
2 Mauricio Delgado, K. Suzanne Scherf and Joshua Smyth, 'The amygdala: An agent of change in adolescent neural networks', *Hormones and Behavior*, 2016, www.ncbi.nlm.nih.gov/pmc/articles/PMC3781589/
3 University of Rochester Medical Center, 'Understanding the teen brain', *Health Encyclopedia*, www.urmc.rochester.edu/encyclopedia/content. aspx?ContentTypeID=1&ContentID=3051
4 Plan International Australia, 'The dream gap: Australian girls' views on gender equality', 2017, www.plan.org.au/~/media/Plan/Documents/Reports/IDG%20 2017/The%20Dream%20Gap_Final
5 Brian Cole, 'An exploration of men's attitudes regarding depression and help-seeking', University of Nebraska – Lincoln, 2013, digitalcommons.unl.edu/cgi/ viewcontent.cgi?article=1172&context=cehsdiss
6 Jonathan Green and Matthew Jakupcak, 'Masculinity and men's self-harm behaviors: Implications for non-suicidal self-injury disorder', *Psychology of Men & Masculinity*, Vol 17 Issue 2, www.apa.org/pubs/journals/features/men-a0039691.pdf
7 Will Courtenay, 'Constructions of masculinity and their influence on men's well-being: A theory of gender and health', *Social Science & Medicine*, Vol 50 Issue 10, 2000, www.ncbi.nlm.nih.gov/pubmed/10741575
8 Richard de Visser and Jonathan Smith, 'Alcohol consumption and masculine identity among young men', *Psychology & Health*, 2007, www.tandfonline.com/ doi/abs/10.1080/14768320600941772
9 Dennis Reidy et al, 'Masculine discrepancy stress, substance use, assault and injury in a survey of US men', BMJ Publishing Group, 2015, injuryprevention.bmj. com/content/early/2015/07/29/injuryprev-2015-041599
10 Exploring Teens, www.exploringteens.com.au
11 The Rite Journey, theritejourney.com/manmade-toolbox/
12 Heejung Park and Jean Twenge, 'The decline in adult activities among U.S. adolescents, 1976–2016', *Child Development*, 2017, onlinelibrary.wiley.com/doi/ abs/10.1111/cdev.12930

Conversation #3 – Love Education

1 Making Caring Common Project, 'The talk: How adults can promote young people's healthy relationships and prevent misogyny and sexual harassment', Harvard University, https://mcc.gse.harvard.edu/thetalk
2 Alan Bailey, Alexandra Parker and Faye Scanlan, 'Adolescent romantic relationships – why are they important? and should they be encouraged or avoided?', Headspace, headspace.org.au/assets/Uploads/Resource-library/Health-

        professionals/romanticrelationships-adolescent-romantic-relationships-why-are-
        they-important-headspace-evsum.pdf
3   Sally Morris, 'Snapshot of mental health and suicide prevention statistics for
        LGBTI people and communities', National LGBTI Health Alliance, 2016,
        lgbtihealth.org.au/resources/snapshot-mental-health-suicide-prevention-statistics-
        lgbti-people and K.H. Robinson et al, 'Growing up queer: Issues facing young
        Australians who are gender variant and sexuality diverse', Young and Well
        Cooperative Research Centre, 2014, www.blackdoginstitute.org.au/about-us/news-
        and-media/mindthefacts
4   Scott Monroe et al, 'Life events and depression in adolescence: Relationship loss
        as a prospective risk factor for first onset of major depressive disorder', *Journal of
        Abnormal Psychology*, 1999, www.ncbi.nlm.nih.gov/pubmed/10609425

Conversation #4 – Choices
1   Parenting Ideas, parentingideas.com.au

Conversation #5 – Body Image
1   Bridianne O'Dea (ed.), 'Social networking sites, depression, and anxiety: A
        systematic review', *JMIR Mental Health*, 2016, www.ncbi.nlm.nih.gov/pmc/
        articles/PMC5143470/
2   Lauren Sherman et al, 'The power of the like in adolescence: Effects
        of peer influence on neural and behavioral responses to social media',
        Psychological Science, Vol 27 Issue 7, 2016, journals.sagepub.com/doi/
        abs/10.1177/0956797616645673
3   RSPH, 'Instagram ranked worst for young people's mental health', Royal Society
        for Public Health, 2017, www.rsph.org.uk/about-us/news/instagram-ranked-worst-
        for-young-people-s-mental-health.html
4   Chiara Rollero and Norma de Piccoli, 'Self-objectification and personal values:
        An exploratory study', *Frontiers in Psychology*, 2017, www.ncbi.nlm.nih.gov/pmc/
        articles/PMC5482001/
5   Derek E. Baird, 'Picture of health: Boys advertising and body image', Credos,
        www.scribd.com/document/321039410/Picture-of-Health-Boys-Advertising-and-
        Body-Image
6   Marla Eisenberg, Dianne Neumark-Sztainer and Melanie Wall, 'Muscle-enhancing
        behaviors among adolescent girls and boys', *American Academy of Pediatrics*, 2012,
        pediatrics.aappublications.org/content/early/2012/11/14/peds.2012-0095
7   Body Matters Australasia, bodymatters.com.au
8   Peter L. Benson, *How Parents Can Help Ignite the Hidden Strengths of Teenagers*,
        Jossey-Bass, 2008

Conversation #6 – Unconditional Love
1   The Rite Journey, theritejourney.com/programs/theparentingplan/
2   Eliza Cook and Rachel Dunifon, 'Do family meals really make a difference?',
        Parenting in Context, Cornell University College of Human Ecology, 2012, www.
        human.cornell.edu/sites/default/files/PAM/Parenting/Family-Mealtimes-2.pdf

Conversation #8 – Media Messages
1   Katie Paciga et al, 'Carrying Fred Rogers' message forward in the digital age',
        Fred Forward Symposium Proceedings, Fred Rogers Center for Early Learning and
        Children's Media at Saint Vincent College, 2017, www.fredrogerscenter.org/wp-
        content/uploads/2015/07/Carrying-Fred-Rogers-Message-Forward-in-the-Digital-
        Age.pdf

2   Digital Nutrition, www.digitalnutrition.com.au
3   Douglas Gentile et al, 'Protective effects of parental monitoring of children's media use', *JAMA Pediatrics*, 2014, jamanetwork.com/journals/jamapediatrics/fullarticle/1852609
4   Sandi Wallace, 'Associations between shared musical engagement and parent–child relational quality: The mediating roles of interpersonal coordination and empathy', *Journal of Family Communication*, Vol 18 Issue 3, 2018, www.tandfonline.com/eprint/eJz5eH7qiMmZCePXHWpE/full

Conversation #9 – Objectification

1   Brené Brown, 'Dehumanizing always starts with language', 2018, brenebrown.com/blog/2018/05/17/dehumanizing-always-starts-with-language/
2   APA Task Force, 'Report of the APA Task Force on the sexualisation of girls', American Psychological Association, 2010, www.apa.org/pi/women/programs/girls/report-full.pdf
3   Australian Psychology Society, 'Submission to NSW Inquiry into the sexualisation of children and young people', 2016, www.psychology.org.au/About-Us/What-we-do/advocacy/Submissions/Public-Interest/Submission-inquiry-sexualisation-of-children
4   Caroline Heldman, 'Sexual objectification, part 1: What is it?', 2012, drcarolineheldman.com/2012/07/02/sexual-objectification-part-1-what-is-it/

Conversation #10 – Sex Education

1   Making Caring Common Project, 'The talk: How adults can promote young people's healthy relationships and prevent misogyny and sexual harassment', Harvard University, https://mcc.gse.harvard.edu/thetalk
2   Youth Work Ireland, 'Young people turn away from teachers and parents and towards the internet for sex education', 2018, www.youthworkireland.ie/what-we-do/news/young-people-turn-away-from-teachers-and-parents-and-towards-the-internet-f
3   Jochen Peter and Patti Valkenburg, 'Adolescents and pornography: A review of 20 years of research', *Journal of Sex Research*, www.ncbi.nlm.nih.gov/pubmed/27105446
4   Lauren Duberstein and Issac Maddow-Zimet, 'Consequences of sex education on teen and young adult sexual behaviors and outcomes', *Journal of Adolescent Health*, 2011, www.ncbi.nlm.nih.gov/pubmed/22999833
5   Henrietta Cook, 'State school under fire for telling students to "delay sexual activity"', *Sydney Morning Herald*, 10 August 2017, www.theage.com.au/victoria/state-school-under-fire-for-telling-students-to-delay-sexual-activity-20170809-gxsmij.html
6   Cicely Marston, 'Anal heterosex among young people and implications for health promotion: A qualitative study in the UK', *BMJ*, 2014, bmjopen.bmj.com/content/4/8/e004996
7   Melinda Tankard Reist, 'Girls as young as 12 to be taught how to send naked images in Victorian schools', 2018, melindatankardreist.com/2018/07/girls-as-young-as-12-to-be-taught-how-to-send-naked-images-in-victorian-schools/
8   Cicely Marston, 'Anal heterosex among young people and implications for health promotion: A qualitative study in the UK', *BMJ*, 2014, bmjopen.bmj.com/content/4/8/e004996
9   Margaret Blythe, 'Incidence and correlates of unwanted sex in relationships of middle and late adolescent women', *Archives of Pediatrics and Adolescent Medicine*, 2006, jamanetwork.com/journals/jamapediatrics/fullarticle/205084

10 Mark Greene, 'Teaching our sons independence above all else is an isolating trap', 2017, medium.com/@remakingmanhood/insisting-boys-learn-independence-above-all-else-creates-an-isolating-trap-for-men-31892c7cba16

11 Bryana French, 'Coerced sex not uncommon for young men, teenage boys, study finds', *American Psychological Association*, 2014, www.apa.org/news/press/releases/2014/03/coerced-sex.aspx

12 Youth Work Ireland, 'Young people turn away from teachers and parents and towards the internet for sex education', 2018, www.youthworkireland.ie/what-we-do/news/young-people-turn-away-from-teachers-and-parents-and-towards-the-internet-f

13 Jean-Yves Frappier et al, 'Sex and sexual health: A survey of Canadian youth and mothers', *Paediatrics and Child Health*, Vol 13 Issue 1, 2008, www.ncbi.nlm.nih.gov/pmc/articles/PMC2528827/

14 Eric Owens et al, 'The impact of internet pornography on adolescents: A review of the research', *Sexual Addiction & Compulsivity*, Vol 19, 2012, www.tandfonline.com/doi/abs/10.1080/10720162.2012.660431?src=recsys&journalCode=usac20

15 Kaye Wellings et al, 'Sexual behaviour in context: A global perspective', *The Lancet*, Vol 369 Issue 9558, 2007, www.sciencedirect.com/science/article/pii/S0140673606694798

16 J. Dennis Fortenberry, 'Sexual development in adolescents', *Handbook of Child and Adolescent Sexuality*, 2013, www.sciencedirect.com/science/article/pii/B9780123877598000076

17 Juliette D. G. Goldman, 'Responding to parental objections to school sexuality education: a selection of 12 objections', *Sexuality, Society and Learning*, 2008, www.tandfonline.com/doi/abs/10.1080/14681810802433952

18 Jeff Hearn, 'Where are the boundaries of sexuality?', *Sexualities*, 2018, journals.sagepub.com/doi/abs/10.1177/1363460718785108?journalCode=sexa

19 Jean M. Twenge and Heejung Park, 'The decline in adult activities among U.S. adolescents, 1976–2016', *Child Development*, 2017, onlinelibrary.wiley.com/doi/abs/10.1111/cdev.12930

20 Youth Risk Behavior Study, 'Trends in the Prevalence of Sexual Behaviors and HIV Testing National YRBS: 1991—2017', CDC, 2017, www.cdc.gov/healthyyouth/data/yrbs/pdf/trends/2017_sexual_trend_yrbs.pdf

21 J. Dennis Fortenberry, 'Sexual development in adolescents', *Handbook of Child and Adolescent Sexuality*, 2013, www.sciencedirect.com/science/article/pii/B9780123877598000076

22 Anne Mitchell et al, 'National Survey of Australian Secondary Students and Sexual Health 2013', Australian Research Centre in Sex, Health and Society, LaTrobe University, 2014, www.latrobe.edu.au/news/articles/2014/release/teen-sexual-health-survey-launched

23 Sexually Transmitted Diseases Surveillance, 'STDs in adolescents and young adults', CDC, 2015, www.cdc.gov/std/stats15/adolescents.htm

24 Debby Herbenick et al, 'Sexual behavior in the United States: Results from a national probability sample of men and women ages 14–94', *Journal of Sexual Medicine*, 2010, onlinelibrary.wiley.com/doi/10.1111/j.1743-6109.2010.02012.x/abstract?deniedAccessCustomisedMessage=&userIsAuthenticated=false

25 Jon Zimmerman, 'We're casual about sex and serious about consent. But is it working?' *The Washington Post*, 13 October 2015, www.washingtonpost.com/news/in-theory/wp/2015/10/13/were-casual-about-sex-and-serious-about-consent-but-is-it-working/

26   Michael Livingston, 'Trends in non-drinking among Australian adolescents', *Society for the Study of Addiction*, 2014, ndarc.med.unsw.edu.au/sites/default/files/newsevents/events/Livingston%20young%20drinkers%20in%20Australia.pdf

27   Jonaki Bose et al, 'Key substance use and mental health indicators in the United States', *SAMHSA*, 2015, www.samhsa.gov/data/sites/default/files/NSDUH-FFR1-2015/NSDUH-FFR1-2015/NSDUH-FFR1-2015.pdf

28   Drinkaware, www.drinkaware.co.uk/advice/underage-drinking/teenage-drinking/

29   Annalisa Belloni, 'Tackling harmful alcohol use', OECD, www.oecd.org/unitedkingdom/Tackling-Harmful-Alcohol-Use-United-Kingdom-en.pdf

30   Jennifer Livingston and Maria Testa, 'Alcohol consumption and women's vulnerability to sexual victimization: Can reducing women's drinking prevent rape?', *Substance Abuse and Misuse*, 2009, www.ncbi.nlm.nih.gov/pmc/articles/PMC2784921/

31   Drug and Alcohol Research and Training Australia, darta.net.au

32   Richard Mattick, 'Association of parental supply of alcohol with adolescent drinking, alcohol-related harms, and alcohol use disorder symptoms: A prospective cohort study', *The Lancet Public Health*, Vol 3 Issue 2, 2018, www.thelancet.com/journals/lanpub/article/PIIS2468-2667(17)30240-2/fulltext

33   Amy Pennay, Michael Livingston and Sarah MacLean, 'Young people are drinking less: It is time to find out why', *Drug and Alcohol Review*, 2015, onlinelibrary.wiley.com/doi/abs/10.1111/dar.12255

34   Richard P. Mattick et al, 'Early parental supply of alcohol: Association with drinking in mid-adolescence?', National Drug and Alcohol Research Centre, UNSW, ndarc.med.unsw.edu.au/sites/default/files/newsevents/events/Parental%20supply%20presentation%20slides.pdf

Conversation #11 – The Hook-up Myth

1   Justin Garcia, 'Sexual hook-up culture', *American Psychological Association*, Vol 44 Issue 2, www.apa.org/monitor/2013/02/ce-corner.aspx

2   Making Caring Common Project, 'The talk: How adults can promote young people's healthy relationships and prevent misogyny and sexual harassment', Harvard University, https://mcc.gse.harvard.edu/thetalk

3   Michael Kimmel, *Guyland: The perilous world where boys become men*, HarperCollins Publishers, 2009

4   Justin Garcia, 'Sexual hook-up culture', *American Psychological Association*, Vol 44 Issue 2, www.apa.org/monitor/2013/02/ce-corner.aspx

5   Murray Lee et al, 'Sexting and young people', Report to the Criminology Research Advisory Council, 2015, www.criminologyresearchcouncil.gov.au/reports/1516/53-1112-FinalReport.pdf

6   Maryland Collaborative to Reduce College Drinking and Related Problems, 'Sexual assault and alcohol: What the research evidence tells us', Center on Young Adult Health and Development, 2016, www.plan.org.au/learn/who-we-are/blog/2016/03/02/dont-send-me-that-pic

7   Anne Mitchell et al, 'National survey of Australian secondary students and sexual health 2013', Australia Research Centre in Sex, Health and Society, LaTrobe University, 2014, www.latrobe.edu.au/news/articles/2014/release/teen-sexual-health-survey-launched

8   Murray Lee et al, 'Sexting among young people: Perceptions and practices', Trends and Issues in Crime and Criminal Justice, www.aic.gov.au/publications/current%20series/tandi/501-520/tandi508.html

9　　Sheri Madigan et al, 'Prevalence of multiple forms of sexting behavior among youth', *JAMA Pediatrics*, 2018, jamanetwork.com/journals/jamapediatrics/fullarticle/2673719

10　Ateret Gewirtz-Meydan et al, 'What do kids think about sexting?', *Computers in Human Behavior*, Vol 86, 2018, www.sciencedirect.com/science/article/pii/S0747563218301699

11　Kidspot Editor, 'Students from 70 Australian schools targeted by sick pornography ring', *Kidspot*, 16 August 2016, www.kidspot.com.au/parenting/real-life/in-the-news/students-from-70-australian-schools-targeted-by-sick-pornography-ring/news-story/ff5b6140865dd3f6f3a1eb531137bece

12　Plan International and Our Watch, '"Don't send me that pic": Online sexual harassment and Australian girls', 2016, www.plan.org.au/learn/who-we-are/blog/2016/03/02/dont-send-me-that-pic

13　Sara Thomas, '"What should I do?": Young women's reported dilemmas with nude photographs', *Sexuality and Social Policy*, Vol 15 Issue 2, 2018, link.springer.com/article/10.1007/s13178-017-0310-0

14　International Justice Mission, ijm.org.au

Conversation #12 – Misogyny and Harassment

1　　Making Caring Common Project, 'The talk: How adults can promote young people's healthy relationships and prevent misogyny and sexual harassment', Harvard University, https://mcc.gse.harvard.edu/thetalk

2　　Making Caring Common Project, '6 tips for parents: Reducing and preventing misogyny and sexual harassment among teens and young adults', Harvard University, mcc.gse.harvard.edu/files/gse-mcc/files/mcc_the_talk_misogynyparenttips.pdf

3　　Holly Kearl, 'The facts behind the #MeToo movement: 2018 study on sexual harassment and assault', Stop Street Harassment, 2018, www.stopstreetharassment.org/resources/2018-national-sexual-abuse-report/

4　　The Line, 'The how-to guide to stepping up against sexist behaviour,' 2015, www.theline.org.au/how-to-guide-to-stepping-up-against-sexist-behaviour

Conversation #13 – Pornography

1　　NSPCC, 'What should I do? NSPCC helplines report about online safety', 2018, www.nspcc.org.uk/services-and-resources/research-and-resources/2016/what-should-i-do-helpline-report-online-abuse/

2　　Chyng Sun et al, 'Pornography and the male sexual script: An analysis of consumption and sexual relations', *Archives of Sexual Behavior*, 2016. www.ncbi.nlm.nih.gov/pubmed/25466233

3　　P. Tomaszewska and B. Krahé, 'Predictors of sexual aggression victimization and perpetration among Polish university students: A longitudinal study', *Archives of Sexual Behavior*, 2018, www.ncbi.nlm.nih.gov/pubmed/27543105

4　　NSPCC, '"I wasn't sure it was normal to watch it"', 2018, www.mdx.ac.uk/__data/assets/pdf_file/0021/223266/MDX-NSPCC-OCC-pornography-report.pdf

5　　Ibid.

6　　Leila Green et al, 'Risks and safety for Australian children on the internet: Full findings from the AU Kids Online survey of 9–16 year olds and their parents', *Cultural Science Journal*, Vol 4 Issue 1, 2011, culturalscience.org/articles/abstract/10.5334/csci.40/

7　　David Finkelhor, Chiara Sabina and Janis Wolak, 'The nature and dynamics of internet pornography exposure for youth', *CyberPsychology and* Behavior, Vol 11 Issue 6, 2008, www-liebertpub-com.ezproxy.uws.edu.au/doi/10.1089/cpb.2007.0179

8   Michael Flood, 'Exposure to pornography among youth in Australia',
     Journal of Sociology, 2007 journals.sagepub.com.ezproxy.uws.edu.au/
     doi/10.1177/1440783307073934

9   David Finkelhor, Chiara Sabina and Janis Wolak, 'The nature and dynamics
     of internet pornography exposure for youth', *CyberPsychology and* Behavior,
     Vol 11 Issue 6, 2008, www-liebertpub-com.ezproxy.uws.edu.au/doi/10.1089/
     cpb.2007.0179

10   Chyng Sun et al, 'Pornography and the male sexual script: An analysis of
     consumption and sexual relations', *Archives of Sexual Behavior*, 2016. www.ncbi.
     nlm.nih.gov/pubmed/25466233

11   NSPCC, '"I wasn't sure it was normal to watch"', 2018, www.mdx.ac.uk/__data/
     assets/pdf_file/0021/223266/MDX-NSPCC-OCC-pornography-report.pdf

12   Michael Flood, 'Exposure to pornography among youth in Australia',
     Journal of Sociology, 2007 journals.sagepub.com.ezproxy.uws.edu.au/
     doi/10.1177/1440783307073934

13   The Henry J. Kaiser Family Foundation, 'Generation Rx.com: How young people
     use the internet for health information', 2001, kaiserfamilyfoundation.files.
     wordpress.com/2001/11/3202-genrx-report.pdf

14   Eric W. Owens et al, 'The impact of internet pornography on adolescents: A
     review of the research', *Sexual Addiction and Compulsivity*, 2012, citeseerx.ist.psu.
     edu/viewdoc/summary?doi=10.1.1.661.1654

15   Meghan Donevan and Magdalena Mattebo, 'The relationship between frequent
     pornography consumption, behaviours, and sexual preoccupancy among
     male adolescents in Sweden', *Sexual and Reproductive Healthcare*, 2017, www.
     sciencedirect.com/sdfe/pdf/download/eid/1-s2.0-S187757561630101X/first-page-pdf

16   NSPCC, '"I wasn't sure it was normal to watch it"', 2018, www.mdx.ac.uk/__data/
     assets/pdf_file/0021/223266/MDX-NSPCC-OCC-pornography-report.pdf

17   Shane W. Kraus and Brenda Russell, 'Early sexual experiences: the role of
     Internet access and sexually explicit material', *CyberPsychology and Behavior*, Vol
     11 Issue 2, 2008, www.ncbi.nlm.nih.gov/pubmed/18422408

18   Linette Etheredge and Janine Lemon, 'Pornography, problem sexual behaviour
     and sibling on sibling sexual violence', *Submission to the Royal Commission into
     Family Violence*, 2015, www.rcfv.com.au/getattachment/B8A6174A-6C6F-495F-
     BF7B-9CA9BF902840/Etheredge,-Linette

19   Barnado's, 'Police figures reveal rise of almost 80% in reports of child-on-
     child sex offences', 2017, www.barnardos.org.uk/news/Police_figures_reveal_
     rise_of_almost_80_in_reports_of_child-on-child_sex_offences/latest-news.
     htm?ref=121581

20   Cyra Fernandes and Russell Pratt, 'How pornography may distort risk
     assessment of children and adolescents who sexually harm', *Interpreting
     Neuroscience, Creating Evidence*, Vol 40 Issue 3, 2015, www.cambridge.
     org/core/journals/children-australia/article/how-pornography-may-
     distort-risk-assessment-of-children-and-adolescents-who-sexually-harm/
     EF8CA41869CF275C623C53995756D108

21   Tiffany Hoyt and Laura R. Ramsey, 'The object of desire: How objectified creates
     sexual pressure for women in heterosexual relationships', *Psychology of Women
     Quarterly*, 2014, journals.sagepub.com/doi/abs/10.1177/0361684314544679

22   L. Monique Ward, 'Media and sexualization: State of empirical research,
     1995–2015', *Journal of Sex Research*, Vol 53 Issue 4-5, 2016, www.tandfonline.com/
     doi/abs/10.1080/00224499.2016.1142496?journalCode=hjsr20

23   Kimberly Mitchell and Michele Ybarra, 'Exposure to internet pornography
     among children and adolescents: A national survey', *Cyberpsychology, Behavior*

and Social Networking, 2005, www-ncbi-nlm-nih-gov.ezproxy.uws.edu.au/pubmed/16232040?dopt=Abstract

24   Suzan Doornwaard, 'Lower psychological well-being and excessive sexual interest predict symptoms of compulsive use of sexually explicit internet material among adolescent boys', *Journal of Youth and Adolescence*, 2015, www.ncbi.nlm.nih.gov/pubmed/26208829

25   Rebecca Guy, John Kaldor and George Patton, 'Internet pornography and adolescent health', *Medical Journal of Australia*, 2012, www.mja.com.au/journal/2012/196/9/internet-pornography-and-adolescent-health

26   Your Brain on Porn, 'Studies linking porn use to poorer mental-emotional health and poorer cognitive outcomes', www.yourbrainonporn.com/studies-linking-porn-use-poorer-mental-cognitive-health

27   Chyng Sun et al, 'Pornography and the male sexual script: An analysis of consumption and sexual relations', *Archives of Sexual Behavior*, 2016. www.ncbi.nlm.nih.gov/pubmed/25466233

28   Brian Y. Park, 'Is internet pornography causing sexual dysfunctions? A review with clinical reports', *Behavioral Sciences*, 2016, www.ncbi.nlm.nih.gov/pmc/articles/PMC5039517/

29   Ibid.

30   Jochen Peter and Patti M. Valkenburg, 'Processes underlying the effects of adolescents' use of sexually explicit internet material: The role of perceived realism', *Communication Research*, 2010, journals.sagepub.com/doi/abs/10.1177/0093650210362464

31   Dolf Zillmann, 'Influence of unrestrained access to erotica on adolescents' and young adults' dispositions toward sexuality', *Journal of Adolescent Health*, Vol 27 Issue 2, 2000, www-sciencedirect-com.ezproxy.uws.edu.au/science/article/pii/S1054139X00001373

32   Chyng Sun et al, 'Pornography and the male sexual script: An analysis of consumption and sexual relations', *Archives of Sexual Behavior*, 2016. www.ncbi.nlm.nih.gov/pubmed/25466233

33   Paul J. Wright, 'Pornography and sexual behavior: Do sexual attitudes mediate or confound?', *Communication Research*, 2018, journals.sagepub.com/doi/abs/10.1177/0093650218796363

34   NSPCC, '"I wasn't sure it was normal to watch"', 2018, www.mdx.ac.uk/__data/assets/pdf_file/0021/223266/MDX-NSPCC-OCC-pornography-report.pdf

35   Johanna M. F. van Oosten et al, 'Adolescents' sexual media use and willingness to engage in casual sex: Differential relations and underlying processes', *Human Communication Research*, 2016, onlinelibrary.wiley.com/doi/abs/10.1111/hcre.12098

36   Scott Braithwaite et al, The influence of pornography on sexual scripts and hooking up among emerging adults in college', *Archives of Sexual Behavior*, 2014, www.ncbi.nlm.nih.gov/pubmed/25239659

37   Lucy Watchirs Smith, 'Is sexual content in new media linked to sexual risk behaviour in young people? A systematic review and meta-analysis', *Sexual Health*, 2016, www.ncbi.nlm.nih.gov/pubmed/27509401

38   Ruth Lewis and Cicely Alice Marston, 'Anal heterosex among young people and implications for health promotion: a qualitative study in the UK', BMJ Open, Vol 4 Issue 8, 2014, bmjopen.bmj.com/content/4/8/e004996

39   Jochen Peter and Patti M. Valkenburg, 'Adolescents and pornography: A review of 20 years of research', *Journal of Sex Research*, 2016, https://www.ncbi.nlm.nih.gov/pubmed/27105446

40   Nicky Stanley et al, 'Pornography, sexual coercion and abuse and
      sexting in young people's intimate relationships: A European study',
      Journal of Interpersonal Violence, 2016, journals.sagepub.com/doi/
      abs/10.1177/0886260516633204

41   Ashley Kraus, Robert S. Tokunaga and Paul J. Wright, 'A meta-analysis of
      pornography consumption and actual acts of sexual aggression in general
      population studies', *Journal of Communication*, 2015, onlinelibrary.wiley.com/doi/
      abs/10.1111/jcom.12201

42   Jochen Peter and Patti M Valkenburg, 'Adolescents' Exposure to a Sexualized
      Media Environment and Their Notions of Women as Sex Objects', *Sex Roles*,
      2007, link.springer.com/article/10.1007/s11199-006-9176-y

43   Gert Martin Held, Theis Lange and Neil N Malamuth, 'Pornography and Sexist
      Attitudes Among Heterosexuals', *Journal of Communication*, 2013, onlinelibrary.
      wiley.com/doi/abs/10.1111/jcom.12037

44   Nicky Stanley et al, 'Pornography, sexual coercion and abuse and sexting in
      young people's intimate relationships: A European study', *Journal of Interpersonal
      Violence*, 2016, journals.sagepub.com/doi/abs/10.1177/0886260516633204

45   Sean Bannon, Matthew W. Brosi and John D. Foubert, 'Pornography viewing
      among fraternity men: Effects on bystander intervention, rape myth acceptance
      and behavioral intent to commit sexual assault', *Sexual Addiction and
      Compulsivity*, 2011, www.tandfonline.com/doi/abs/10.1080/10720162.2011.625552

46   Tatsuhiko Ikeda, Ken-Ichi Ohbuchi and Goya Takeuchi, 'Effects of
      violent pornography upon viewer's rape myth beliefs: A study of Japanese
      males', *Psychology, Crime and Law*, 2008, www.tandfonline.com/doi/
      abs/10.1080/10683169408411937?journalCode=gpcl20

47   Todd Love et al, 'Neuroscience of Internet pornography addiction: A review and
      update', *Behavioral Sciences*, Vol 5 Issue 3, 2015, www.ncbi.nlm.nih.gov/pmc/
      articles/PMC4600144/

48   Ewelina Kowalewska, 'Neurocognitive mechanisms in compulsive sexual
      behavior disorder', *Current Sexual Health Reports*, 2018, www.researchgate.net/
      publication/327979092_Neurocognitive_mechanisms_in_compulsive_sexual_
      behavior_disorder

49   Porn Study Critiques, 'Brain studies on porn users and sex addicts', 2015,
      pornstudycritiques.com/current-list-of-brain-studies-on-porn-users/

50   Michael Flood, *'Inquiry into the harm being done to Australian children through
      access to pornography on the internet'*, 2016, www.echildhood.org/statement

51   *Eric W. Owens et al, The impact of internet pornography on adolescents: A review
      of the research'*, Sexual Addiction and Compulsivity, www.tandfonline.com/doi/
      abs/10.1080/10720162.2012.660431?src=recsys&journalCode=usac20

52   *Youth Work Ireland, 'Young people turn away from teachers and parents and towards
      the internet for sex education'*, 2018, www.youthworkireland.ie/what-we-do/news/
      young-people-turn-away-from-teachers-and-parents-and-towards-the-internet-f

53   Ibid.

54   Ryan M. Atwood, 'Adolescent problematic digital behaviors associated with
      mobile devices', *North American Journal of Psychology*, Vol 19 Issue 3, 2017,
      search.proquest.com/openview/c5fc95bb175a31002888f87fdd4333ff/1?pq-
      origsite=gscholar&cbl=28796

55   Lian McGuire and James O'Higgins Norman, 'Cyberbullying in Ireland',
      National Anti-Bullying Research and Resource Centre, Dublin City University,
      2016, www.dcu.ie/sites/default/files/institute_of_education/pdfs/ABC-
      Cyberbullying-Survey.pdf

56   Australian Psychological Society, 'Teens need more guidance using social media to avoid harm, psychologists say', 2017, psychology.org.au/About-Us/news-and-media/Media-releases/2017/Teens-need-more-guidance-using-social-media-to-avo
57   Beáta Bóthe et al, 'The development of the Problematic Pornography Consumption Scale (PPCS)', *The Journal of Sex Research*, 2017, www.researchgate.net/publication/313400277_The_Development_of_the_Problematic_Pornography_Consumption_Scale_PPCS

Conversation #14 – Manners and Helping

1   Jean Illsley Clarke, Kris Loubert and Wendy Wicks, 'Involving children in household tasks: Is it worth the effort?', College of Education and Human Development, University of Minnesota, 2014, ww1.prweb.com/prfiles/2014/02/22/11608927/children-with-chores-at-home-University-of-Minnesota.pdf
2   Resilient Youth, '90% of young Australians want to help others', 2017, www.resilientyouth.org.au/blog/young-australian-students-want-to-help-others
3   Thomas G. Plante, 'Helping others offers surprising benefits', *Psychology Today*, www.psychologytoday.com/blog/do-the-right-thing/201207/helping-others-offers-surprising-benefits-0
4   Lara Aknin, J. Kiley Hamlin and Elizabeth Dunn, 'Giving leads to happiness in young cildren', *PLOS*, journals.plos.org/plosone/article?id=10.1371/journal.pone.0039211

Conversation #15 – Empathy

1   Making Caring Common Project, Harvard University, mcc.gse.harvard.edu
2   Making Caring Common Project, 'MCC Research Report', Harvard University, mcc.gse.harvard.edu/files/gse-mcc/files/mcc-research-report.pdf?m=1448057487
3   P. Tomaszewska and B. Krahé, 'Predictors of sexual aggression victimization and perpetration among Polish university students: A longitudinal study', *Archives of Sexual Behavior*, 2018, www.ncbi.nlm.nih.gov/pubmed/27543105
4   Daniel Goleman, *Emotional Intelligence*, Random House, 2005

My Conversation with Schools

1   Australian Psychology Association, 'Submission to the Senate Environment and Communications References Committee Inquiry into the harm being done to Australian children through access to pornography on the internet', 2013, https://www.psychology.org.au/getmedia/2f794e03-996e-4230-bbaf-5288e21016bd/Submission-australian-children-accessing-pornography.pdf
2   Making Caring Common Project, 'The talk: How adults can promote young people's healthy relationships and prevent misogyny and sexual harassment', https://mcc.gse.harvard.edu/thetalk
3   Australian Psychology Society, 'Submission to the Senate Environment and Communications References Committee Inquiry into the harm being done to Australian children through access to pornography on the internet', 2016, https://www.nspcc.org.uk/preventing-abuse/keeping-children-safe/online-porn/
4   The Rite Journey, theritejourney.com

INDEX